C000141425

Secret Wartime Britain

Secret Wartime Britain

Hidden Places That Helped Win The Second World War

Colin Philpott

Pen & Sword
MILITARY

First published in Great Britain in 2018
and reprinted in this format in 2020 and 2021 by
Pen & Sword Military
An imprint of
Pen & Sword Books Ltd
Yorkshire – Philadelphia

Copyright © Colin Philpott 2018, 2020, 2021

ISBN 978 1 52677 494 1

The right of Colin Philpott to be identified as Author of this work has been
asserted by him in accordance with the Copyright, Designs and Patents Act 1988.

A CIP catalogue record for this book is
available from the British Library.

All rights reserved. No part of this book may be reproduced or transmitted in any
form or by any means, electronic or mechanical including photocopying, recording
or by any information storage and retrieval system, without permission from the
Publisher in writing.

Printed and bound in England by CPI Group (UK) Ltd, Croydon, CR0 4YY

Pen & Sword Books Limited incorporates the imprints of Atlas, Archaeology,
Aviation, Discovery, Family History, Fiction, History, Maritime, Military,
Military Classics, Politics, Select, Transport, True Crime, Air World, Frontline
Publishing, Leo Cooper, Remember When, Seaforth Publishing, The Praetorian
Press, Wharncliffe Local History, Wharncliffe Transport, Wharncliffe True Crime
and White Owl.

For a complete list of Pen & Sword titles please contact

PEN & SWORD BOOKS LIMITED
47 Church Street, Barnsley, South Yorkshire, S70 2AS, England
E-mail: enquiries@pen-and-sword.co.uk
Website: www.pen-and-sword.co.uk

Or
PEN AND SWORD BOOKS
1950 Lawrence Rd, Havertown, PA 19083, USA
E-mail: Uspen-and-sword@casematepublishers.com
Website: www.penandswordbooks.com

This book is dedicated to my parents' and grandparents' generations across the world who had to live through all this.

Contents

Introduction

Aerial masts of the Chain Home Radar Station near Worth Matravers on the Isle of Purbeck in Dorset, which was the centre of British radar research from 1940 until 1942. (Purbeck Radar Museum Trust)

Two particular experiences inspired me to write this book. While walking the Dorset section of the South West Coastal Path, I came across a place that was new to me – the barely visible remains of the Chain Home Radar Station near Worth Matravers not far from Swanage. This was a vast, hastily-constructed radar station set on the cliff tops overlooking the English Channel. It played a key role in the development of radar which gave the Allies a crucial advantage in the air war with Germany, yet it was just one of thousands of places either built from scratch or fashioned from existing buildings which were pressed into service in the Second World War in the desperate struggle for victory over Nazi Germany. The story of how and why these places were built, what contribution they made to the war effort and what has happened to them after 1945, seemed to me a fascinating one worth telling.

The second experience was even more poignant. It was hearing the stories of people like Evelyn Philp who, as a young woman during the war, worked at the Avro aircraft factory next to what is now Leeds-Bradford Airport in West Yorkshire. She was one of over 10,000 people working there at the height of the war on a shift system which involved twenty-four-hour continuous production. Most of the workers were women and most were conscripted to work at the factory which built almost 700 Lancaster bombers, 4,500 Avro-Ansons and other planes and made a major contribution to the country's wartime production.

What I found most remarkable about the story of the Avro Factory and of Evelyn Philp was that, despite its vast size, the factory was never bombed. In addition, the overwhelming majority of Evelyn and her colleagues, who had all signed the Official Secrets Act, never spoke about what they did there. In some cases they remained silent for many years after the war. I was keen to understand more about why people did apparently keep quiet about what they did at these locations and how important that was for the successful prosecution of the war.

Production line inside the Avro factory near Leeds where 4,500 Avro-Astons and 695 Lancasters, as well as other planes, were produced during the war. (Leeds Library and Information Services)

So, this is a story about both places and people and this book sets out to do two things. It seeks to provide an overview of the largely secret places in Second World War Britain and to tell some of their individual stories. Why were they needed? Why were the particular locations chosen? What were the problems and challenges of getting them built or adapted for war use? Who were the people who worked there and the people who conceived, planned and organised these places?

In telling this story, I am not aiming to be encyclopaedic – there are simply too many places. However, I will try to cover all the main categories of places under the following headings –factories; command centres; spying and listening bases; broadcasting and propaganda locations; a section on dummy and decoy sites and D-Day deceptions designed to confuse German bombers and intelligence; a chapter on retreats and reserves, including places used by the British Resistance and the stores for the nation's art treasures; interrogation and detention centres, including a look at how people who gave away secrets were punished and finally, a visit to the places where Britain researched and made the deadliest of weapons. Within each category, I have attempted to give examples of places rather than try to list them all and, where possible, I have tried to find people associated with the locations and to hear their stories.

The second objective of this book is to examine the secrecy which, to a greater or lesser extent, surrounded these places, most of which, incidentally, were not buried beneath ground. How secret were these locations? How, and indeed, whether the secrecy was maintained? How much did the Germans know? Why does it appear that these places did remain largely hidden from view – either literally or metaphorically? And, perhaps most importantly, why was it that ordinary people did apparently respond positively to the 'Careless Talk Costs Lives' message and kept quiet about what they did – a silence which many maintained long after victory had been achieved, and which some even took to their graves? Was it the threat of punishment? Was it the effectiveness of propaganda? Was it the fact that mid-twentieth century Britain was still a very hierarchical and deferential society? Was it simply perhaps the case that people knew that they were engaged in an existential struggle?

This is a story which, of course, has to be set in a wider context. Firstly, the military context of the position Britain and her allies found themselves in when attempts to avert war failed in 1939. The popular view is that Britain was ill-prepared to face the well-organised military might of Germany. The traditional narrative tells us that Britain was the plucky underdog who survived against the odds until the Americans were finally persuaded to join the fight.

Recently, this view has come under scrutiny from revisionist historians who have argued that Britain was better prepared than often thought, and the Germans less so. Nevertheless, it was undoubtedly the case that, certainly for the first three or four years of the war, arguably longer, victory was by no means assured. After the retreat of British forces from the beaches of Dunkirk, and during the relentless German bombardment of British cities during 1940 and 1941, the outlook was pretty bleak. Against this backdrop, it would not perhaps be surprising that the vast majority of Britons pulled together, part of which included, to use the slang of the time, 'Keeping Mum' about things which might benefit the enemy.

An anti-rumour and 'Careless Talk' poster, one of many produced by the Ministry of Information for their campaigns throughout the war. (National Archives)

The second important context was the reality of the home front during the Second World War which was the first major conflict in human history which fully involved the civilian populations at home as well as the military on the front line. In 1939 ordinary Britons were expecting mass aerial bombardment of their towns and cities – a fear which proved to be fully justified. They also feared chemical attacks and were all issued with gas masks – a fear which, fortunately, proved to be groundless. These fears, along with the dislocations caused by the absence of loved ones in the armed forces and the evacuation of young children, brought the reality of war very close to everyone in their daily lives. Again, this provides a very plausible reason why people might have maintained silence and discretion in what they knew was a fight for survival.

Thirdly, it is easy to forget now just how much wartime Britain in the 1940s was a centralised, highly planned and regulated country with strict censorship, identity cards and with sweeping powers given to government officials to conduct the war without many of the normal constraints on state power which existed in a peacetime democracy. Ironically, many of the freedoms for which Britain was fighting were at least partially suspended during a conflict undertaken to preserve democracy. On top of this, a great deal of effort was expended by government and other organs of the state into propaganda to get people to behave in a way that would allow the best possible pursuit of the country's war aims. So, even those people who might have been less willing to support the war and the privations and restrictions it brought, were perhaps more likely to toe the line because the penalties for not doing so were significant or because they had been persuaded by clever propaganda to fall into line.

Fourthly, there is another important aspect of the traditional narrative of the Second World War from the British perspective that feeds into this story. I think it is fair to say that a great deal of the British sense of the war is based on the notion that the Allies won as much because of superior cunning as superior military might. British literature, film and television are very keen on tales of canny Brits outsmarting the brutal but rather plodding Germans. So, the deception around the D-Day landings, the exploits of the Bletchley Park codebreakers, the turning of German agents, the activities of the Special Operations Executive behind enemy lines and many other examples are still widely hailed as proof of British intellectual genius and our ruthless use of deception, intrigue and cunning without which the war might have been lost. I have little doubt that all these things did contribute to the Allied victory but there is perhaps a bit of a tendency to overplay this.

Nevertheless, it is a significant context for the story of secrecy within Britain during the war.

In summary, therefore, I hope to come to some conclusions about the role of all these factors – the military reality, the impact of mass bombing, the effectiveness of censorship, government controls and propaganda, and the apparent British love of deception and cunning – in the story of Britain's secret wartime locations and the many places and people that were part of it. I shall pay particular attention to two key pieces of evidence – the extent to which key 'secret' locations were hit by bombing, and the number of people brought before the courts for 'Careless Talk' offences under the wartime regulations.

The Second World War retains a very strong hold on the collective British psyche. I suppose this is due to several factors – some of the generation who fought in its battles are still alive, many of the generation that experienced

The flooded remains of 'The Paddock', the alternative underground bunker built in Dollis Hill in north-west London as a back-up for the Cabinet War Rooms in Whitehall. (Colin Philpott)

the home front as children (the generation of my parents) are still very much with us; and, of course, the war is still a key part of the curriculum in our schools so that even those generations born long after it happened have an awareness of what it was all about.

Above all, though, maybe we still enjoy talking about and learning more about the war because it can be portrayed by Britons as a morally unambiguous struggle. There is no doubt that there was a real and present danger against which Britain had to defend itself. More than that, it was a struggle principally against a demonstrably evil philosophy and regime, that of Nazi Germany and fascism more generally, of which the world needed to be rid. Subsequent wars in which this country has been involved, for example in Iraq and Afghanistan, have generally been seen as less clear cut in their justification and, in some cases, have been pursued by our leaders in the face of widespread popular opposition. So, it is easy to see why the Second World War remains a hunting ground for historians, authors and, it should be said, for politicians who wish to use it as justification for this or that contemporary policy.

The moral realities of the Second World War were of course rather less straightforward than they are often portrayed. The mass bombing of German and Japanese cities by Britain and its Allies was, to say the least, morally questionable and to some constituted a war crime. The failure of Britain and its Allies to try to stop the Holocaust despite incontrovertible evidence of awareness of it still rankles. Although Britain (and the United States) by and large abided by the Geneva Convention and other 'rules of war' in their prosecution of the conflict, chemical weapons were made and stored by the Allies and, of course, the atom bomb was developed and used. And a reasonable argument can be made that many British politicians of the time were themselves guilty of some aspects of the racism, anti-Semitism, and authoritarianism which characterised the Nazis.

Nevertheless, most people then and now would accept, albeit reluctantly, that the Second World War was a conflict which Britain had to fight both as a matter of self-defence and as a matter of human rights. It is in that context that I believe that the story of secrecy on the home front during that war is worth telling. It helps to illuminate what people went through at the time and throws some light on understanding the outcome of the conflict. Also, it probably tells us something about how much the world has changed in the three generations since.

It seems almost inconceivable to those of us living in the social media age of the early twenty-first century that people engaged in secret work could keep quiet about what they did. It seems difficult to comprehend how people remained silent about vast factories that appeared in their neighbourhoods. It defies our belief that those in possession of information about military knowledge kept their mouths shut. The story of how and why they apparently did is a story not just about politicians, boffins and generals, but about ordinary people and ordinary everyday places in what was Secret Wartime Britain.

Chapter One

Factories

Vera Stobbs' Secret Life at a Royal Ordnance Factory;
Ammunition Dumps and Explosions; the Shadow Factories of Coventry;
the Camouflaging of Avro Leeds; 1,000s of factories hidden in plain sight;
'Folly' Factories Underground

Royal Ordnance Factory, Newton Aycliffe, County Durham

At the age of 94, Vera Stobbs recalled the events of three-quarters of a century ago as though they were yesterday. As an 18 year old, she started work in 1942 at the Royal Ordnance Factory at what was then Aycliffe in County Durham. Vera spoke to me in early 2018, just a few months before her death, about her experiences there. She spoke proudly and fondly of her time there, but it was a tough life which in many ways robbed her of the best years of her youth. A year before starting at the factory her mother had died and it fell to her, given the gender roles of the era, to look after her father who was a miner. Her caring responsibilities meant that she was able to avoid night shifts at the factory. However, she still had to work a relentless six-day-a-week pattern of either early or late shifts, six in the morning until two in the afternoon, or two in the afternoon until ten at night. It was dull, monotonous work and she had to keep the home functioning as well once she had finished.

Vera's job was to inspect detonators. She had to open boxes, check the detonators and make sure they had been correctly assembled. She did this over and over again throughout her shift with just one half-hour break. She remembers a man she calls 'The Commander' coming round each shift to check on their work. Not only was the work boring and repetitive, it was also dangerous. Working with explosive materials brought obvious hazards and one of her friends, Rosie, died in an explosion in the very room where Vera worked, but on a shift when she was off-duty. There were several accidents at the factory during the course of the war. The worst, in May 1945, just days before the end of the conflict, claimed eight lives and an earlier blast, in February 1942, resulted in the deaths of four women.

Vera Stobbs, one of the 'Aycliffe Angels' who worked at ROF59, the Royal Ordnance Factory at Aycliffe in County Durham from 1942 until the end of the war. (Colin Philpott)

When I spoke to Vera in 2018 at her home in what is now Newton Aycliffe, the new town built after the war near the site of the factory, she told me that she didn't really appreciate the danger of the work at the time. It was just something in the background and she didn't think about it all the time. However, there were plenty of warnings in the form of notices and instructions from factory bosses about the risks. Workers were reminded that carelessness could result in explosions in the factory causing injury or death to them and their colleagues, but also mistakes might lead to faulty munitions finding their way to the battlefront with terrible consequences there.

The factory was divided into a 'clean side' where the most volatile materials were handled and where restrictions were tightest and a 'dirty side' where things were a bit more relaxed. However, as part of the precautions taken to minimise the risk of explosions or chemical incidents, all workers

One of the few buildings still remaining from the Royal Ordnance Factory site at Aycliffe in County Durham and which now forms part of the Newton Aycliffe Industrial Estate. (Colin Philpott)

had to wear special shoes and overalls which they put on at the beginning of each shift. They were checked to make sure they didn't have any flammable items in their possession, like matches and cigarettes, or metal objects like hair grips which might fall into machinery.

As well as the risk of explosion, there were a variety of dangers to health to those working in munitions factories. The materials involved in the manufacture of armaments often caused skin and hair to turn yellow (munitions workers were referred to as 'canaries'), caused asthma and breathing problems, sometimes made teeth fall out and even damaged the lining of the stomach. Vera Stobbs was lucky enough to escape these problems, but many of her fellow-workers did suffer significant health issues.

An even greater potential danger came not from within the factory but from the skies above – the risk of German aerial bombardment – and it was against this risk that a range of measures were taken to protect the factory. First of all, its location was deliberately chosen. The Royal Ordnance Factory, Aycliffe, known by its code number of ROF59, was opened in 1941 covering a site of 857 acres and eventually employing over 17,000 people in around 1,000 separate buildings. The site, then in largely open countryside between Darlington and Bishop Auckland, was apparently selected because it was in low-lying ground which was often misty and cloudy. In addition, many wartime factories were built away from main centres of population and away from what was regarded as the more vulnerable south-east of England.

Like many similar factories, ROF59 was camouflaged both by painting and also with the planting of grass on the roofs of the buildings. However, it was a vast site protected by barbed-wire fences and it was impossible to conceal it completely – a characteristic shared with many vital Second World War facilities in Britain.

The site was well-guarded. Most workers arrived either by bike, bus or train at special stations close to the factory. All workers needed a pass and there were armed police at the gate. Vera Stobbs says she has no recollection of having had to sign the Official Secrets Act, nor does she remember any particular instructions about keeping quiet about the work. However, she never spoke to anyone outside the factory about what she did there during the war. She believes that people just knew instinctively that they should keep quiet about it and that the vast majority of her colleagues thought the same. This is a view that I heard many times in the conversations I had on this subject. Vera also pointed out that the site was remote and that, although most of the people who worked there lived in neighbouring large towns like Darlington and Bishop Auckland, it was nevertheless a close-knit

Mrs Skinner clocks on for her shift at a munitions factory, somewhere in Britain, 1940. A large group of her fellow workers are lined up behind her to punch their work card when their turn arrives. (Imperial War Museum)

community and most of the ROF workers did not meet many other people from outside so opportunities to 'blab' were limited, even if workers had been so inclined.

If there were any breaches of security, their effect was limited. There are claims that German spies infiltrated the factory. William Joyce, the British traitor, who broadcast on an English language radio station from Germany under the name 'Lord Haw-Haw', is said to have made reference to the factory in one of his broadcasts. He promised that the factory would be bombed and that 'those little Angels of Aycliffe won't get away with it'. But even if, as seems likely, the Germans were aware of the factory, it was never bombed. Vera Stobbs doesn't recall ever having to go into the factory's air raid shelters during the day shifts there, although there were air attacks in the area and some bombs did drop nearby. Overall, a combination of its location, its camouflage, its security and the secrecy apparently maintained there meant that it was hidden in plain sight, a characteristic shared by so many of the locations to be encountered on this journey.

The survival of ROF Aycliffe without being bombed, like many other similar factories, was of enormous importance to the war effort. It was what was known as a 'filling factory'. Its main role was to put powder into shells and bullets and to assemble detonators and fuses. The official history of wartime ordnance factories published at the end of the war estimated that the factory produced seven million bullets during the conflict so it made a major contribution to Britain's wartime production effort. It was a contribution which was largely down to women who made up 85 per cent of the workforce. Indeed, the epithet 'Aycliffe Angels' originating from the Lord Haw-Haw broadcast, was adopted to describe the workforce at Aycliffe.

One of the most important aspects of the story of Second World War Britain is the contribution of women on the home front – a contribution which many feel has never received the credit it deserves. Women were encouraged to volunteer from the start of the war and by 1941 more than

A group photograph of workers at the Royal Ordnance Factory at Aycliffe, County Durham. They became known as the 'Aycliffe Angels' after William Joyce, aka 'Lord Haw-Haw' referred to them as such during a broadcast threatening to bomb the factory. (Vera Stobbs)

a million were involved in the Women's Voluntary Service (WVS) helping with tasks such as evacuation and assistance for victims of bomb damage. However, it soon became clear that women would also be needed in the armed services and in so-called essential occupations – work deemed to be vital to the war effort like factories and farming.

The call-up of women started in 1941. At first it affected just single women aged 20 to 30 but eventually 90 per cent of single women and 80 per cent of married women were involved in the armed forces, factories or on the land. Talking to Vera Stobbs and to others who worked in factories, they were immensely proud of what they did and they enjoyed the companionship and friendships formed during the war years. Although the work was dull and dangerous, the Aycliffe Angels had fun there. Vera told me about the 'best ankles' competitions the women organised to relieve the boredom. She recalled the dark humour of playing jokes by getting on stretchers to try to convince the managers that accidents had happened.

One of the remaining buildings at the former Royal Ordnance Factory at Aycliffe has been turned into a war-themed activity centre known as ROF59 (Colin Philpott)

However, Vera and many of the women who had worked there, and their families, felt that it took far too long for there to be sufficient recognition for their efforts. Winston Churchill made a morale-boosting visit to the factory on 15 May 1942 but in the post-war narrative of the Allies' victory, it was usually the frontline efforts of Battle of Britain pilots and others which tended to be given most prominence. The contribution of the millions of people, the vast majority of them women, who worked on war production, was often overlooked. In the 1980s and 1990s there was renewed interest in the story of ROF Aycliffe and a campaign started for recognition. Eventually, a memorial plaque was erected in the centre of Newton Aycliffe. Moreover, in 2010 an All Party Parliamentary Group on Recognition of Munitions Workers was set up by a group of British MPs with a view to improving official recognition for the contribution of munitions workers during the war.

Meanwhile, the site of ROF59 had been transformed from 1946 onwards into the Newton Aycliffe Industrial Estate. Many of the factory buildings were redeveloped for peacetime industrial use. One building became the new headquarters of Durham Police. By 2018 most of the original buildings had disappeared to be replaced by new units. However, some remain and, in one of them, a new business – a fitness and indoor climbing centre complete with Blitz Restaurant and Bunker Bar – has opened called ROF 59. It maintains the wartime theme and original notices from the 1940s can be seen on the walls.

Other Munitions Factories

ROF Aycliffe was just one of fifty-one munitions factories across Britain during the Second World War. There were four categories of factories – the engineering factories producing casings for bombs and shells and weapons; small-arms factories making bullet casings; explosive factories manufacturing explosive agents and finally, the filling factories like Aycliffe which filled the bomb and shell casings with explosive substances. Some of these factories were run by private companies that had switched their premises from producing civilian consumer goods to war production; many of the factories were built and run by the Government.

Prior to 1939 Britain's armaments production had been concentrated mainly on three factories in or near London – the Royal Arsenal at Woolwich, the Royal Gunpowder Factory at Waltham Forest and the Royal Small Arms Factory at Enfield, as well as a small number of factories elsewhere. However, the likelihood of mass aerial bombing necessitated moving munitions production away from the most vulnerable part of the country – London and the south-east. Most munitions factories were therefore built west of a line running roughly from the Bristol Channel to the Tyne. In selecting sites, the key factors were remoteness from areas most vulnerable to bombing, but with reasonable proximity to available supplies of labour and to transport links.

The biggest and the most dangerous were the filling factories like Aycliffe. The factory at **Bridgend** in South Wales was said to be the largest factory in Britain at the time of its construction in the late thirties. When it was fully operational by March 1940, it covered over 1,000 acres and eventually employed more than 32,000 at its peak during 1942. Officially, seventeen people died in accidents there. Like Aycliffe, it was situated on reclaimed marshland and often shrouded in mist. After the war parts of the site were bulldozed, parts turned into industrial units and others into housing.

ROF Swynnerton near Stone in Staffordshire was another massive site, also a filling factory and, like Aycliffe and Bridgend, chosen partly because it was in an area prone to mist. Started in 1939, the factory was operational the following year and reached peak employment in 1942 with 18,000 working there, mostly women between 18 and 35 years old. The majority of workers were local but Swynnerton, like some other munitions factories, also employed women from all over the country and accommodation hostels were built to house them. The factory had its own railway station which never appeared in any rail timetable.

Swynnerton had more than 2,000 separate buildings. This type of dispersal was typical of the munitions factories in an attempt to reduce the risk of explosions in one area causing damage across the wider facility. After the war many of Swynnerton's buildings had to be destroyed because they were contaminated with dangerous chemicals, but the site remained a factory until 1958. Later it became, and remains to this day, an army training camp. In 2017 Swynnerton was announced as a possible site for a new 'garden village' with 10,000 homes.

ROF Chorley in Lancashire employed 28,000 workers at its peak. Bouncing bombs, used in the celebrated Dambusters raids, were filled at Chorley. The site had an extensive network of underground storage tunnels known as **ROF Heapey**. After the war, pre-fabricated houses were built on the Chorley site, but it continued its role as a munitions factory; later as part of BAE, until 2009. In 2018 the site had various uses – partly housing, partly industrial and partly as a college, but the underground storage facility still exists although run by a private company.

Among other notable ordnance factories were **ROF Thorp Arch near Wetherby** in West Yorkshire. Today part of the site is occupied by

The remains of part of ROF Bishopton in Renfrewshire in 2015 during redevelopment of the site for housing and a business park. (Thomas Nugent)

the British Library's Northern Reading Room and major storage facility. **ROF Bishopton** in Renfrewshire manufactured cordite, employed 20,000 people and continued as a factory into the twenty-first century. Today, it has partly been redeveloped as housing and a business park. An example of an armaments factory run by a private company on behalf of the government was the factory at **Charlesfield** near St Boswells in Roxburghshire. It was one of two factories, the other being in Kilmarnock, producing incendiary bombs from 1942 to 1945. It is claimed that between them the two factories produced 90million bombs. Today the site is a business park.

Ammunition Dumps

As well as places to manufacture armaments, sites were needed to store the products of Britain's munitions factories. In the late 1930s such facilities were in very short supply. By 1938 a strategy had been developed which was intended to protect as much as possible of the country's ammunition supplies from the risk of bombing. This involved building a few underground sites spread around the country as well as above ground dumps close to airfields. Five main sites were developed as underground stores:

Corsham Central Ammunition Depot, Wiltshire. The extensive underground complex, carved from nineteenth century quarries beneath the Wiltshire village of Corsham, later become the most iconic of Cold War locations in Britain as the alternative centre of national government in the event of nuclear attack. However, its first government use was as an ammunition store in the Second World War. In 1936 the War Office completed the purchase of the Ridge, Tunnel and Eastlays Quarries and in 1937 added an additional area – the Monkton Farleigh quarry. These were developed at a cost of around £4.5million (about £188million at 2018 prices). Around 300,000 tonnes of explosives were able to be stored there. At first winches were used to lower the explosives into the stores, but later railway lines and conveyor belts transported the ammunition. The first ammunition arrived in 1938. There were problems with maintaining the correct temperature and humidity for the safe storage of highly flammable materials and air-conditioning systems had to be installed.

The security and secrecy of the site was taken very seriously. During the construction of the depot, it is believed that rumours were deliberately put about that a massive underground food dump was being built to try to disguise the true purpose of the new facility. The depot was extensively guarded by a combination of regular military and Home Guard. With the quarries 30 metres below ground, the real risk was not to the stores themselves but to the railway lines and yards above ground which supplied the stores. Decoy and dummy sites were developed to confuse the Luftwaffe (see Chapter Five). All of this seems to have been successful with only two recorded instances of bombs nearby. Both of these occurred in August 1940 – one caused negligible damage and in the other, bombs almost certainly intended for a nearby airfield, landed harmlessly in fields near the depot.

RAF Fauld near Hanbury in Staffordshire has acquired a macabre celebrity as the place where Britain's biggest explosion took place on 27 November 1944 when 3,670 tonnes of bombs, weapons and other materials exploded in the underground store. Two giant plumes of smoke could be seen for miles around and a crater half-a-mile across was left by the explosion which broke a nearby dam and destroyed an entire farm and several other buildings. The precise death toll is not known but it is believed that about seventy people died in the accident – many of them were above ground and not working in the store. The cause is thought to have been the use of a brass chisel rather than a wooden baton to remove a detonator from a live bomb. Remarkably, parts of the underground store survived the explosion. After the war the RAF continued to use the site as a store until 1966. Later it was used by the US Army. Since 1979 the area has been returned to nature, although some explosives are believed to have been left buried underground as they were deemed too dangerous to move.

The three other underground stores were at **Chilmark in Wiltshire, Llanberis in North Wales** and at **Harpur Hill in Derbyshire**. The Llanberis store suffered a calamitous collapse in January 1942 when 14,000 tonnes of bombs were buried – representing at the time about 14 per cent of the RAF's total stock. Most of this stock was recovered but Llanberis was never used again for underground storage.

Inside the former ammunition store at Llanberis in North Wales where there was a major ground collapse in January 1942. An estimated 14 per cent of the RAF's total ammunition supplies were held there at the time. (Nick Catford)

In addition to these underground stores there were, by the end of the war, scores of ammunition dumps known as Ammunition Parks and later Forward Filling Stations for the RAF, Royal Navy and Army around Britain. An example of these was the **Broughton Moor** site near Maryport on the Cumbrian coast. In 1938 the former colliery site was converted into an arms store for the Royal Navy, covering 850 acres and later extended to 1,050 acres. Eleven people died and seventy were injured in an explosion there in 1944. After the war the site was used by the West German Government and later by the US for the storage of explosive materials.

Overall, the business of making and storing the ammunition needed by Britain during the Second World War was a massive undertaking involving millions of people, hundreds of locations across Britain and significant dangers to life and limb.

Coventry – A Case Study In Wartime Production

The city of Coventry has an iconic resonance in the story of Second World War Britain. The picture of its ancient cathedral ruinously bombed by the Luftwaffe is one of the defining images of the conflict. The 'Big Raid' of 14/15 November 1940 not only cost nearly 600 people their lives and left the city centre devastated, it also moved the horror of the war to a higher level of terror in the British consciousness. From that point onwards, the concept of 'total war' involving virtually the whole civilian population in many parts of Britain, not just London, became a reality.

Coventry's suffering was not confined to the night of the infamous 'Moonlight Sonata' raid. It was attacked no fewer than forty-seven times and, relative to its size, it was one of the most bombed of all British cities. The principal reason for attracting such interest from German bombers was its importance as a centre of wartime production. An estimated total of around a hundred factories, both large and small, were involved in making weaponry of one sort or another and it was therefore not surprising that it was so heavily targeted in German air raids.

If the story of developing Britain's wartime munitions capacity was characterised by a rather last-minute scrambling, the efforts to build up Britain's aircraft production were underway earlier and Coventry played a leading role in that. The development of the Shadow Factory Scheme from 1935 was a direct consequence of the debate running through much of the 1930s about the threat of aerial bombardment. Britain had experienced a taste of such bombardment in the latter stages of the First World War

Damage caused by an air raid on the Rootes No 1 Factory at Aldermoor Lane in Coventry, a city where an estimated 100 factories were involved in wartime production (Rootes Collection at the Coventry Archives and Research Centre)

and the development of military aircraft after that (including the bombing of towns during the Spanish Civil War) had induced a widespread dread among politicians and people alike – a fear which was probably comparable to present day anxiety of nuclear attack. Also prevalent in the Thirties was a certain resigned fatalism about the risks of bombing summed up in a speech to the House of Commons by the British Prime Minister, Stanley Baldwin, as early as 1932 in which he said:

'I think it is well also for the man in the street to realise that there is no power on earth that can protect him from being bombed. Whatever people may tell him, the bomber will always get through.

The only defence is in offence, which means that you have to kill more women and children more quickly than the enemy if you want to save yourselves...'

It was this view that influenced the development of Britain's air strength even before war with Nazi Germany became all but certain in late 1938. Later, of course, as we shall discover, the rather defeatist view that defences against bombing were largely futile was changed with great effect. However, the emphasis of government thinking and military planning prior to 1939 was to build up Britain's ability to strike at an enemy from the air.

The idea of the Shadow Factory Scheme was to utilise the skills and expertise of existing engineering companies to boost Britain's capacity for aircraft production. The Government would partner with a number of private companies and build, at public expense, new factories close to the location of the company's existing production facilities. The private companies would manage the 'shadows' alongside their original factories and learn the skills required for adapting their expertise to the needs of military aircraft manufacture.

Three companies based in Coventry were selected for the first wave of shadow factories – Standard, Rootes and Daimler. Standard's shadow was built at Banner Lane on the western outskirts of the city; Daimler's at Browns Lane to the north and Rootes' at Ryton, just outside the city boundaries to the south-east.

Interestingly, the selection of the locations was decided in discussions between the Ministry of Aircraft Production and the companies without any consultation with Coventry City Council. The council's archives from the time reveal how cross local councillors felt about this. They also record how councillors and local landowners, whose greenbelt property was to be compulsorily purchased for the scheme, raised concerns about the impact of building the factories in Coventry.

In one exchange of letters, a solicitor representing a local landowner accused government officials in these terms in May 1939: 'The Ministry can wreck the town planning work of the Corporation since its inception and alter the layout and possibly the consequent history of the City for all time.'

It was only eighteen months later that the Luftwaffe altered the layout of Coventry rather more dramatically! However, what this comment does show is that, even with war imminent, the regrettable necessities of war production were perhaps not fully appreciated.

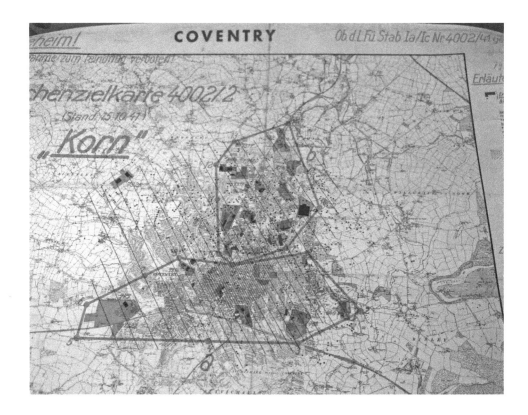

Map produced by the Luftwaffe showing the location of factories and other key installations in Coventry and using 'Korn' – the Germans' code name for Coventry. (Coventry Archives and Research Centre)

The Council also had serious concerns about the practical impact that building the shadow factories would have on the city's infrastructure. As the three new factories were either built or under construction in 1939, it was estimated that as many as 35,000 extra workers would be needed in Coventry. With some of these workers bringing their families with them, Coventry was to need extra accommodation for as many as 50,000 people – representing a 20 per cent increase in the city's population. Correspondence between the Town Clerk and various Government ministries shows that Coventry's local politicians clearly believed that ministries were unsympathetic to their worries about the impact on the local infrastructure – housing, the supply of utilities, roads and local transport to serve the new factories.

Equally, the Government's frustration at Coventry's protestations came through clearly in a letter to the Town Clerk from Sir John Nixon of the Ministry of Aircraft Production in July 1940: 'I should like to know more about the position of the housing programme. Is there a time schedule yet? It's houses we want – not paper.'

Nevertheless, the factories were built, additional housing was constructed and extra vehicles found to provide factory transport. The main activity of all three factories was the building of aero engines. Bristol Hercules engines were made at the Standard shadow factory at Banner Lane, which was the biggest of the three, built on 88 acres of farmland and employing 6,000 people when it opened.

But these three shadows were a small proportion of the contribution made by Coventry's industrial production to the war effort. It is estimated that one hundred factories, many of them quite small, were involved in war production in one way or another in the city – most of them involved in aero engines, machine tools or military vehicles. Some of the best-known included Armstrong-Siddeley, Singer, Alvis and British Thomson-Houston (BTH). Eventually, the principal factories of Rootes, Daimler and Standard were also given over to war production as well as their shadows.

It was impossible to conceal these factories. Although the main shadow factories were away from the city centre, they were huge. Once the war was underway they were camouflaged, as were many other pre-existing factories. Some were protected by dummy factories designed to confuse enemy bombers.

As well as the bombing, the other threats to the security of the factories were sabotage and leaks of information about the exact nature of what was being produced in each plant. All the factories were guarded, mainly by a specially created police force designed to do this, and there were security checks and identity cards for all workers. In addition, there is strong evidence that the vast majority of those who worked in Coventry's wartime factories, and the factories of other places, did not 'spill the beans' about what they were doing. In part this was down to clear and forceful reminders issued by managers. For example, one worker, in a 1938 account of working life in a Coventry shadow factory, described what his boss had said to him when he started work there:

'Now, look here, you are working in a Government factory. Don't talk to anybody and everybody about the job because practically every perisher in Europe wants to know what's going on here. And, above all, don't tell anyone how many men work here or how fast you work.'

It was a message that clearly got through. The same worker said:

> 'When we leave our jobs, we never think of discussing with the other fellows, what we've been doing all day because somebody will put two and two together and unravel shadow secrets which, for the safety of our country, must remain secret.'

Margaret Allen's father, Tom Hutt, spent thirty years at Samuel Gill and Sons joining at the age of fourteen in 1938 as an apprentice. He worked as a universal grinder on aircraft engine components right through the war. Margaret recalls her father telling her that there was high security at the factory. He was searched on leaving work at the end of each shift to make sure he wasn't taking any components out of the factory. He was required to sign the Official Secrets Act and he remembered how RAF people visited the factory each week to check up on their work.

As well as the strong messages given to workers, it is important to remember that work in many wartime factories was very specialised. Factory workers stayed in their particular section and often had no detailed knowledge of what happened elsewhere in the factory. This helped reduce the danger of information leaking out even if someone was inclined to 'blab'.

What's more, even though the wartime authorities tried to maintain a sense of secrecy around many wartime factories, there had also been deliberate attempts to publicise their existence before the war. On 10 March 1938, King George VI visited five Midlands shadow factories and his visit was given extensive newspaper coverage. More remarkably, Erhard Milch, the Chief Administrator of the Luftwaffe, was given a tour of one Coventry shadow factory in 1937. All of this was, of course, designed to demonstrate to the Germans the strength of Britain's aircraft production capacity.

Therefore, the idea that shadow and other factories in Coventry and elsewhere were really secret is a bit fanciful. Even without the overt publicising pre-war, it wouldn't have taken much for the Germans to work out the most likely concentrations of wartime production factories. A Luftwaffe map of Coventry from October 1941 shows a pretty detailed and accurate knowledge of the location of many factories in the city.

Perhaps the really remarkable conclusion about Coventry's wartime factories is that there was so little real interruption of production despite the Luftwaffe's intense interest in the city. A total of forty-seven air raids are recorded as having been made on Coventry between 25 June 1940 and

Part of the machine shop at the Rootes No 2 Shadow Factory at Ryton near Coventry which later became a Peugeot factory and is now a business park. (Rootes Collection at the Coventry Archives and Research Centre)

3 August 1942. Factories were badly hit in some of these raids. For example, on 12 September 1940, Daimler, GEC and Armstrong-Siddeley were hit with the loss of twenty-eight lives. On 16 September 1940 Standard's main factory was dive-bombed by a single aircraft causing severe damage to the paint shop. In October 1940 a series of raids caused damage to the Daimler, Rover, Singer, Courtaulds and other plants.

On the night of 14/15 November 1940, the 'Moonlight Sonata' raid claimed 568 deaths, 863 serious injuries, destroyed over 4,000 homes and caused damage to two-thirds of Coventry's buildings, leaving the historic city centre including the cathedral in ruins. It is estimated that eighty of the approximately one hundred factories in Coventry were damaged in some way. Triumph and the GEC cable works were destroyed and several others were badly damaged. However, the initial assessment reported to the War Cabinet four days after the raid suggested that the damage to munitions production in the city was less extensive than feared. In many cases, damage was superficial, for example to roofs, with vital machinery unaffected.

The city's infrastructure of supplies, particularly water and power, was severely compromised. It was this which disrupted production in the immediate aftermath of the 'Big Raid' more than damage to the factories themselves. However, supplies were restored relatively quickly and repairs were made to factories such that by Christmas the vast majority of the city's industrial capacity had been restored. As a result of the Coventry raid, an Emergency Services Organisation was set up which acted as a sort of repair flying squad which helped restore damaged factories across the country at great speed.

Today, the sites of the three specially-built Coventry shadow factories are no longer hives of manufacturing. However, after the war, all three acquired new civilian manufacturing roles. The Rootes plant at Ryton, still

The site of the former Standard shadow factory at Banner Lane on the outskirts of Coventry which, after the war, eventually became a Massey Ferguson tractor factory, but which is now redeveloped for housing and shops. (Colin Philpott)

bearing its camouflage into the 1980s, became a Peugeot factory and is now a business park; Standard's Banner Lane factory was the home of Massey Ferguson tractors until it was redeveloped for housing and retail and the Brown's Lane plant of Daimler became Jaguar until it closed in 2007. It now contains housing and a new industrial park was completed in 2017. As you walk around these sites now, it is hard to imagine that, seventy-five years ago, tens of thousands of people were working there round the clock to make the machines which helped turn the war in favour of the Allies.

Avro Factory, Leeds

For several years my regular journey to work took me past a nondescript building obscured by trees not far from Leeds-Bradford Airport. It is now the Leeds-Bradford Airport Industrial Estate and in January 2018 I had the opportunity to go inside the vast edifice. It is a single-storey building of quite extraordinary size now sub-divided into sixteen units and used as warehousing and storage. Its tenants include some of Britain's best-known high street brands. Forklift trucks buzz around the place shifting twenty-first century consumer goods piled high on pallets awaiting delivery by fleets of lorries pulling up in the carpark outside.

Perhaps the most poignant part of the place is the now abandoned entrance hall and stairway which led to the administration offices of the factory when it was opened by Avro for aircraft production in February 1941. Standing here in 2018 amid the faded 1940s décor, it is easy to be transported back to the atmosphere of wartime Britain and imagine what it must have been like to come here each day and work on vital war work under the constant threat of aerial bombardment.

It was not strictly a shadow factory even though it was run by Avro as an offshoot of their main factory at Chadderton in Manchester. Avro Leeds was, however, an example of another important characteristic of wartime production in Britain, the dispersal of capacity. The strategy was to disperse production across a number of sites so that if one were hit, others could continue. Avro Leeds made a major contribution to Britain's wartime aircraft production producing 695 Lancaster bombers, 4,500 Avro-Astons and a number of other types of plane.

An estimated 17,000 people worked at the factory throughout the war with 10,000 working there at one time at its peak. They worked sixty-nine-hour weeks; 60 per cent of the workforce were women and most were conscripts. Most of the workers came from the Leeds and Bradford

The Avro factory is now converted into warehousing but its 1940s reception hall and office area still remains largely as it must have looked during the Second World War. (Colin Philpott)

conurbations although some were conscripted from further afield. As many as 150 buses were used daily to transport workers to the factory. There was compulsory billeting of Avro workers at homes in the neighbouring areas of Yeadon, Rawdon and Guiseley. Householders with spare rooms were required by wartime regulations to make them available. In addition, there were three newly-built housing developments to accommodate the extra workers coming into the area to work at Avro. A total of 300 bungalows were built by the Ministry of Aircraft Production on the Westfield Estate at Yeadon and at Nunroyd in Guiseley as well as a hostel for 700 single people in Horsforth.

In its four years of wartime operation Avro Leeds was never bombed, despite its size. On completion, it was 530 metres long, 225 metres wide, a single storey continuous structure of brick and reinforced concrete with blast walls on the inside offering some protection from air attacks. Its

The highly camouflaged Avro aircraft factory near to what is now Leeds-Bradford Airport was the largest single-span factory space in Europe at the time of its construction in 1940. (Gerald Myers)

140,724 square metres floor area (over 1.5million square feet) is thought to have made it the largest single-span factory in Europe at the time.

However, probably the most significant fact about its construction was its camouflage. Different camouflage was employed at different factories depending on their importance. Some were simply painted in colours designed to minimise reflection and the chances of being spotted, many were covered in netting. But some like Avro at Leeds had more elaborate measures. The skills and expertise of the pre-war film industry were employed on the task, both at Avro and elsewhere, under the auspices of the Camouflage Development and Training Centre established at Farnham Castle in Surrey. These specialists worked with local people to create grassed banks at a forty-five degrees angle along the sides of the building up to the level of the roof. The roof itself was also grassed and made to look like the adjacent farmland, complete with imitation farm buildings, duck ponds, dummy animals and mock bushes and hedges. These features were moved around and altered to reflect the seasons. The camouflaging cost £20,000 (about £800,000 at 2018 prices).

The camouflaging clearly contributed to the fact that the factory escaped any direct hits, although it seems that the Luftwaffe tried to target it. When air raid sirens sounded over the Leeds and Bradford areas on the night of 27 and 28 August 1942, Leslie Briggs and colleagues had to head for the air raid shelters. Leslie told Gerald Myers for his book *Mother Worked at Avro* that he could not stand the claustrophobic atmosphere of the shelter and went outside and lay on the grass observing the German planes overhead. Three passed over and one appeared to circle the factory but then moved away towards the centre of Leeds. Many years later, by an astonishing coincidence, Leslie, who had been in the RAF, met the German pilot who had been flying that plane back in August 1942 and he confirmed that the factory had been the intended target, but they hadn't been able to find it. By that point in the war, Luftwaffe pilots were largely relying on visual observation as Britain had been able to jam the German radio navigation system.

In 2018 there was no one still alive who was well enough and able to talk about their work at Avro Leeds. However, conversations with people whose parents worked there confirm that it was a hard-working environment, but also a place where there was a strong sense of camaraderie. Like many other factories, the Entertainments National Service Association, better known as ENSA, put on concerts in the factory canteen with Gracie Fields among the wartime stars known to have performed there. There was also a morale-boosting visit by the King and Queen on 26 March 1942.

Andy Philp's parents, Jack and Evelyn Philp, met while they were both working at the factory. Jack, who died in 2012, was a sentry but later got a job inside welding and bolting parts of Lancaster bombers. Evelyn, who died at the age of 94 in 2017, also worked on Lancasters assembling electrical components for the cockpit. Jack never spoke to his family about his war experience but Evelyn often recalled the camaraderie of the factory as well as the long hours (often twelve-hour shifts) and the hard work.

After the end of the war, aircraft production continued at the factory but on 18 April 1946, a stunned and angry meeting of workers was told that it would be closing. The *Wharfedale and Airedale Observer* reported the news with dismay and suggested that:

> It would be a scandal if the sheds, tools and other equipment, should be allowed to become derelict. Yeadon, if it cannot go on producing aircraft, should be allowed to go on producing products of value to the community.

The Avro factory now has modern cladding and roofing but its vast footprint remains the same as it was in the 1940s. (Colin Philpott)

By September 1946 production had ceased. Most workers did find other jobs and after various post-war plans came and went, the factory was bought in 1969 and has been developed progressively in the half a century since as an industrial estate within the original building.

Gerald Myers, who spoke to a number of Avro workers back in the 1980s and 1990s, recalls that their natural assumption at the time they worked there was not to discuss the details of what they were doing. He puts it down to three factors – the very different attitudes to authority that existed in the 1930s and 1940s, where it was much less likely that people would question being told to keep secrets; the widely-held determination to win the war; and also a strong sense of not wanting to endanger the boys on the front line, and they were mainly boys, by 'Careless Talk'. However, the idea that the Avro Factory at Leeds, and many others like it, were truly secret is not credible. Its survival was more down to a combination of camouflage and decoy facilities which thwarted the Luftwaffe's attempts to pinpoint its precise location.

Other Wartime Factories

It is difficult to come up with a definitive number of production factories in Second World War Britain but the total ran into thousands. David Rogers, in his study of wartime production factories, lists eighty-two shadow factories but these were only a fraction of the total number of war factories. The Home Office 'Chronicle of Main Air Attacks and their effects on Vital War Effort, 1939 to 1945' records a peak total of 4,988 war factories in 1942 as well as a further 414 ordnance factories. The vast majority of these were existing factories requisitioned for the war effort; very few were newly built. A wide variety of locations were utilised in a many parts of the country. These included:

Castle Bromwich Plant, Birmingham was one of the first and most important of the shadow factories. It was built by the Government but intended to be run by the Nuffield organisation, headed by Lord Nuffield, which owned Morris Motors. When Churchill appointed Lord Beaverbrook as Minister of Aircraft Production in 1940, he was concerned by the delays in finishing the construction and the poor state of labour relations there. Lord Nuffield was made to hand over control to the Ministry, new management was installed and the factory went on to be a key centre for building Spitfires and Lancasters. The site is now the Jaguar plant.

The Lion Works, Newtown in Powys, Wales employed 3,000 at its peak and was managed by Accles and Pollock from Oldbury in the West Midlands. The site was chosen because it was well away from likely bombing targets but the area had a good supply of labour. It manufactured steel for aircraft assembly lines and also other components for aircraft and for guns. It is now a business park.

Airspeed at Christchurch in Dorset managed a shadow factory built on the edge of Christchurch Airfield in 1940, which made Oxford training aircraft and later Horsa gliders and where 695 Horsas were built and assembled. The factory continued building aircraft post-war until 1962. It is now an industrial estate.

The shadow factory built on the edge of Christchurch Airfield in 1940 which made Oxford training aircraft and later Horsa gliders, seen just after the end of the war. (Friends of the New Forest Airfields)

Hillington, Glasgow. Rolls Royce ran this factory as a shadow on the outskirts of Glasgow adjacent to the Renfrew Aerodrome, producing Merlin aero engines for Spitfires, Hurricanes and other aircraft. Rolls Royce continued to use the site until 2005. It is now a business park.

Plessey, Wanstead, London. Plesseys established a factory in an unfinished section of the Central Line of the London Underground between Wanstead and Gant's Hill. It opened in 1942, employed 7,000 people, mainly women, and made machinery for bombers and for code-breaking devices used at Bletchley Park and elsewhere.

Going Underground

There were a number of air raids which completely destroyed or severely impaired wartime factories. Two of the most devastating occurred early in the war in September 1940. On 4 September, 83 people died and 419 were injured in a raid on the Vickers factory near Brooklands racetrack at Weybridge in Surrey where Wellington bombers were being built. One hundred died later in the month when the Spitfire factory in Southampton was flattened by bombs.

It was in the aftermath of these attacks, and at a time when German aerial bombardment was starting to impinge on many parts of Britain, that the idea of building underground factories was first mooted. Lord Beaverbrook, who had been appointed by Churchill as Minister for Aircraft Production in May 1940, became convinced that it was necessary to find suitable locations for constructing vast underground aircraft factories safe from the reach of the Luftwaffe.

A variety of potential locations were considered including using tunnels below Birmingham, abandoned limestone workings under Dudley Zoo and the use of unopened, incomplete sections of the London Underground. Eventually, efforts were concentrated on two main sites – **Spring**

The abandoned tunnels of Drakelow near Kidderminster which became an underground Rover shadow factory in 1942 and which later became a Cold War Regional Seat of Government. (Alex Lomas)

Quarry at Corsham in Wiltshire and **Drakelow at Kidderminster in Worcestershire.** The Spring Quarry plan was to use part of the vast underground complex of workings below Wiltshire to provide an underground shadow factory for the Bristol Aircraft Company's works at Filton in Bristol. The quarry could provide 200,000 square metres of factory space below ground, sufficient to house the entire Filton plant. The project was beset by a series of engineering problems, cost over-runs and a series of changes of plan. Work started on building the new facility in 1941.

However, by the time the first aircraft production began in 1943, the threat of large-scale disruption to aircraft production had substantially reduced as the Allies had by then secured air superiority over the Germans. In the end, Spring Quarry proved to be an expensive and unnecessary project. The original cost had been estimated at £2.3million but the project eventually cost an estimated £13million (just over £1bn at 2018 values). In total 100,932 Bristol aircraft engines were built throughout the war, but only 523 at Spring Quarry.

The Drakelow plan was approved in June 1941 authorising the building of an underground shadow factory for Rover at Blakeshall Common north of Kidderminster. Rover already ran six shadow factories and other factories, mainly in the Midlands and the north of England. This new underground facility with 26,400 square metres of space organised on a grid system was designed to provide back-up for existing factories in Birmingham. Work started in 1941 but the construction was difficult with cost over-runs and accidents which cost seven lives. By the time the factory was ready in 1943, the threat that it was designed to counter was much reduced. In the end, Rover only took up half the space and other parts of the underground complex were put to other uses. After the war, Drakelow became a Cold War Regional Seat of Government bunker until the 1990s. Since 1993 it has been managed by the Drakelow Preservation Trust and it is possible to visit the site on guided tours.

Factories – The Final Reckoning

Towards the end of the war in 1944, 55 per cent of Britain's national income was devoted to defence, compared with just 6 per cent back in 1938. By 1944, 22million Britons were employed either in the armed forces or in wartime industrial production. When the conflict ended, Britain's national debt was around £21bn (equivalent to £800bn in 2018 values) and represented 200 per cent of the country's annual GDP – a much higher proportion, incidentally, than after the financial crash early in the current century.

This vast expenditure on people and resources paid off. Factories were targeted by the Luftwaffe and there was damage to the country's industrial infrastructure. The Home Office produced weekly statistics of air attacks on vital war infrastructure. Their reports listed a total of 8,030 'key point installations' at the peak of the war in 1944. These included approximately 4,000 factories as well as railway sites, ports, power stations and a range of other facilities vital to the war effort. Of the 8,030 key sites overall, there were a total of 4,664 recorded attacks on 2,135 of those sites, so roughly a quarter were hit, some of them more than once. Within those totals, there were 2,615 attacks on 1,328 factories.

These totals demonstrate that the number of Luftwaffe attacks on key installations was high, but what the figures conceal is the impact of these attacks. Overall, despite the damage and the loss of life (60,595 British civilians were killed in air and rocket attacks during the war), the disruption to production was rather less dramatic. Time and time again, as you read the weekly summary reports of air raid damage, you see phrases like 'No disruption to production', 'Minimal impact on production', 'Production resumed within two days', or similar. It is important to remember these were official reports prepared for the War Cabinet and others at the time to provide accurate, unvarnished information rather than for the purposes of propaganda.

The combined effect of the dispersal of production, the establishment after the Coventry 'Big Raid' in November 1940 of the Emergency Services Organisation, and the achievement of Allied air superiority over the Germans by late 1942, reduced the impact of aerial bombardment on war production. Only thirty-five wartime factories were completely destroyed and put out of action permanently throughout the whole course of the war. The impact on the infrastructure on which factories depended was also relatively modest – 39 per cent of all attacks on rail installations had no effect, only 3 per cent of such attacks caused disruption that lasted more than a week. Steel production and the supply of oil and electricity was largely kept intact other than for relatively temporary periods.

Overall, therefore, it is right to conclude that Britain's wartime production capacity was remarkably resilient.

Chapter Two

Command Centres

*Uxbridge's Battle of Britain bunker; Western Approaches Command,
Liverpool; Dover Castle at Dunkirk and D-Day; Special Operations Bases;
Other Command Centres; Churchill's War Room*

Battle of Britain Bunker, Uxbridge, London

Joan Fanshawe played a crucial role on one of the most defining days in twentieth-century history. A member of the Women's Auxiliary Air Force (WAAF), she was on duty at the No.11 Group Operations Room at RAF Uxbridge in West London on 15 September 1940. Joan was a plotter and it was her job to mark on the control map the location of aircraft formations, both German and British, on the basis of information that came in via teleprinter. This was done by using long croupier-style sticks to push wooden blocks that signified the presence of formations in particular grid squares. This was crucial information for the commanders gathered in the underground command bunker who were deciding how to respond to waves of Luftwaffe planes heading for London. Above the map, there was a so-called Tote Board where the resources available to each of the airfields within No.11 Group's area were listed, including planes in the air, planes on the ground and available, and planes under repair and unavailable. She recalled:

> 'It was extremely busy and it was very difficult to find space on the map to put your plot as there was so much activity. But it was crucial you got the position right as decisions were being made on the basis of what I did.'

She remembered 15 September in particular:

> 'We were supposed to change watches at 12, but it used to get a bit chaotic when we changed and on that day Churchill was watching from the observation room above the plotting table, so we couldn't change then and I stayed on for an extra hour.'

The bunker from which much of the Battle of Britain was conducted, the 'plotting room' at RAF Uxbridge and the headquarters of No.11 Group of RAF Fighter Command, has been left to look as it did on 15 September 1940. (Battle of Britain Bunker, Hillingdon Council)

Joan, who worked in the Operations Room from July to October 1940, also reflected on the historical significance of what she did:

'I was extremely young during the Battle of Britain and I didn't really see the bigger picture. I just concentrated on what I had to do, although I did worry about the fact that my parents lived in Hastings and I imagined that all these aircraft would be flying over their house. It was only much later after the war that I realised how important it all was. It was a mercy that Hitler switched from bombing our airfields to bombing London. If he had carried on bombing airfields, we would have run out of fighters and we would have been finished.'

No.11 Group Operations Room at Uxbridge was the nerve centre for command and control of the Battle of Britain fought out in the skies of south-east England in the summer and early autumn of 1940. RAF Fighter Command was split into four groups. No.10 Group covered the South-West of England and South Wales; No.11 Group, commanded by Air Vice-Marshal Keith Park, was responsible for London and the South-East; No.12 Group looked after the Midlands and North Wales; and No.13 Group covered the North of England, Scotland and Northern Ireland. Although all played a role in the battle, it was No.11 Group which bore the brunt of the action, with London and the south-east in the forefront of the attentions of German planes.

No.11 Group Operations Room controlled a series of seven sectors each, containing several airfields across the south-east including some of the most famous names in RAF history – Biggin Hill, Northolt, Tangmere, Kenley and Debden. No.11 Group answered to the overall Fighter Command HQ based at Bentley Priory (see below).

The place where history was made, and the course of the war changed, lay deep underground, hidden from view, and its crucial role apparently unknown to everyone other than those who worked there and those with the highest security clearance. The operations room for No.11 Group, known by those who worked there as 'The Hole', was built between February and August 1939 and was operational just before war was declared on 3 September 1939. RAF Uxbridge had been the operational command centre for the air defence of Great Britain as a whole since 1925. After a reorganisation of the structure of the air defences, No.11 Group was formed in 1936 to be based at Uxbridge, while other RAF command centres were established elsewhere. By that time, the above ground wooden structure which housed the operations room had been deemed unfit for purpose and vulnerable to the threat of bombing.

Making the new operations room secure and keeping it secret was a high priority and was achieved in several ways. RAF Uxbridge was never an operational airfield. It was an administrative centre, so there were no runways to attract attention. Hillingdon House, the original stately home of the estate that existed there before it was bought by the Government during the First World War, still stood on part of the site. There was significant tree cover around where the bunker was built. The new operations room was built 20 metres below ground and it was gas-proof. So, from the air, this vital nerve centre for the defence of Britain would not have been particularly conspicuous and would probably have looked much like a country estate.

During construction, the site had been guarded very carefully and even those working on digging out the ground were apparently unaware of the purpose of their work.

Once the operations room was in use, security for staff working there was strict. Everyone needed a pass and they had to pass through two guarded checkpoints – firstly to get onto the site and also to get into the underground bunker itself. The security post inside the outer door of the bunker can still be seen at the top of the stairs leading down to the operational area. Apparently on one occasion a security guard shot someone at the entrance to the bunker, but it is believed to have been an accident. The operations room at Uxbridge was staffed entirely by service personnel and guarded by military police. Everyone who worked there had to sign the Official Secrets Act and there were regular briefings from senior commanders about the need for secrecy.

The ground level entrance to the Battle of Britain Bunker at RAF Uxbridge which was buried 20 metres below ground and heavily guarded. (Harrison 49)

Perhaps the most dramatic evidence of the precautions taken to maintain secrecy came during VIP visits to the bunker. Winston Churchill visited three times during the Battle of Britain and on numerous other occasions, during which the control room map and Tote Board were fully visible. Churchill, as Prime Minister, was of course fully security-cleared. However, when the King and Queen visited, a curtain was drawn down over the Tote Board temporarily to protect the detailed information about the strength of airpower.

According to Dan Stirland, the Curator of the Battle of Britain bunker, there is no evidence that its true purpose was ever revealed during the war itself. He says that the Germans are known to have made reconnaissance flights over RAF Uxbridge. A number of bombs landed on or near there during the Battle of Britain, causing neither casualties nor anything other than superficial damage. It is not known whether the bunker was the intended target. If the operations room had been taken out of commission by a successful attack, there were backup facilities – at the RAF base at Leighton Buzzard in Bedfordshire (where training took place for the RAF operations room 'plotters' like Joan Fanshawe).

As it was, the security of the Operations Room was maintained and during those crucial months of the Battle of Britain in 1940, it was there that vital decisions were taken in the deployment of RAF resources against the threat of the Luftwaffe. The bunker at Uxbridge was a key part of the Dowding System of air defence. Developed by Air Chief Marshal Hugh Dowding, the Commander of RAF Fighter Command, the system was the world's first integrated air defence intelligence network. It relied on a network of Chain Home radar stations and Royal Observer Corps visual observations (see Chapter Three) to detect enemy aircraft. This information was then transmitted to Bentley Priory by a dedicated landline telephone network which was safer, quicker and more secure than radio communications. It enabled the overall Fighter Command to have a clear picture of the entire UK airspace. With this, they were able to inform the relevant Group Operations Room of Luftwaffe formations. It was then down to the Group Commander to deploy the appropriate resources from their sectors to intercept the German bombers. Before the war, an interception rate of up to 50 per cent was considered good but, with the Dowding System, rates averaged over 90per cent.

The Battle of Britain raged over the skies of southern England from the middle of July 1940 until October. The battle followed the swift German advances through the Low Countries and France earlier that summer and

Air Chief Marshal Hugh Dowding, the Commander of RAF Fighter Command, developed the Dowding System, the world's first integrated air defence intelligence network, which was crucial to the outcome of the Battle of Britain. (Imperial War Museum)

the British retreat from the beaches of Dunkirk at the end of May and beginning of June. With France occupied and the United States still neutral, Britain's position looked bleak. The German objective was to force Britain out of the war either by a negotiated surrender or by invasion. During the battle, the Luftwaffe targeted Britain's fighter aircraft by attacking their airfields, its radar system, its industrial infrastructure and eventually its civilian population.

A total of 2,937 RAF or Fleet Air Arm pilots are recorded as having taken part in the Battle of Britain of whom 544 were killed. German air crew losses were greater. An estimated 1,733 German aircraft were shot down. By the end of the battle, the threat of imminent German invasion of Britain had disappeared.

It is said that Churchill, at the end of one of his visits to No.11 Group Operations Room on 16 August 1940, first uttered one of his most famous phrases, 'Never in the field of human conflict has so much been owed by so many to so few', a phrase he was to repeat four days later in the House of Commons.

Later in the war, the bunker at Uxbridge played a role in co-ordinating air support for the D-Day landings in June 1944. After the war, it continued as the operational RAF command centre for the south-east of England and was still used as a communications base into the 1970s. The historic map room was first reconstructed in 1975 and made to look as it would have done on 15 September 1940. A museum was opened in the bunker in 1985 and booked tours of the site first started. In 2018 a new museum was opened above ground to explain the story of the site more fully.

Standing in the Operations Room today, three-quarters of a century after the Battle of Britain, is a poignant experience. Imagining the atmosphere 20 metres below ground back in the summer of 1940 with the RAF commanders and the WAAF 'plotters' making split second decisions which could cost or save lives, is very awe-inspiring. Imagining Churchill and other VIPs observing all this in real time from the 'royal box' observation room above the map table is similarly iconic. As we look back with the benefit of hindsight, the outcome may feel inevitable but to those involved, it was anything but.

Western Approaches Command Centre, Liverpool

The exploits of RAF fighter and bomber pilots and those who directed them on the ground have generally hogged the limelight of Britain's Second World

War military history, and understandably so. Yet the Allies' eventual victory probably owes as much, if not more, to the Atlantic convoys of merchant ships and the naval craft that protected them. The Battle of the Atlantic was arguably the decisive struggle of the war. Had the vital supply line from the United States been severed by German U-boats, Britain would have been denied both military hardware, but also food. It could quite literally have been starved into submission.

The secret location from which such a crucial battle was directed for much of the war is a perfect example of somewhere 'hidden in plain sight', a recurring theme of this book. The fact that such momentous events, which changed the course of history, were plotted beneath an ordinary office block in a city centre street somehow adds to the mystique and glamour of the achievements of those who worked there.

Derby House, as it was then known, was an unfinished office block just a few hundred metres from the banks of the River Mersey in the centre of Liverpool. It was surveyed as a possible command centre during the late 1930s but it only came into use in February 1941 when the Western Approaches Command operations room moved there from Plymouth. The underground complex had walls one metre thick and a roof two metres thick. It was bomb proof and gas proof. There were five levels below ground, more than a hundred rooms and between 300 and 400 people worked there. It is believed that the bunker was created by converting what had been intended as an underground restaurant.

During the first two years of the war, Combined Operations, a joint Royal Navy and RAF command controlling the Battle of the Atlantic, had been based in Plymouth. However, a safer and more central location was deemed necessary. One option was a base on the Clyde, but Liverpool was chosen and Derby House was acquired, its basement strengthened and converted for the role. Liverpool was a logical choice as it was the most important port for the Atlantic convoys. More than 1,000 convoy ships docked there bringing vital supplies from the other side of the Atlantic. An estimated 90 per cent of transatlantic cargo arrived via Liverpool. The port of Liverpool was also an important repair yard.

As a result of this strategic importance, Liverpool and its surroundings were a key German bombing target. An estimated 4,000 people died in bombing raids in Merseyside during the war and there was extensive damage to the city. Apart from London, Liverpool was the most bombed city in Britain with regular raids from 1940 until 1942.

Below ground, however, protected inside what staff knew as the 'Citadel' or the 'Fortress', shifts of naval and air force commanders, and shifts of

An anonymous looking office building in the centre of Liverpool under which was built the Western Approaches Command bunker from where the Battle of the Atlantic was directed from February 1941 until the end of the war. (Colin Philpott)

Wrens (Women's Royal Naval Service) and WAAFs worked round the clock. They kept tabs on the movement of Britain's merchant fleet and its naval protectors, as well as the aircraft involved in protecting this vital shipping. In the main map room, a giant plan of the Atlantic was used to plot the position of ships and, more importantly, of the German U-boats trying to destroy them. A white marker on the map indicated the estimated position of a U-boat. A black marker showed a confirmed position. Much of the information which was conveyed to Western Approaches Command came as a result of intelligence gathered through the breaking of German naval codes at Bletchley Park.

A crucial characteristic of the operation at Derby House was the joint working of the Royal Navy and the RAF in the same combined control room. Traditional rivalries were put aside and the two services worked closely together with great effect. This inter-service collaboration was a key feature of much of the British and wider Allied conduct of the war, something generally not replicated by the German services.

Stella Passey, a Wren who worked as a messenger at Western Approaches Command, recalled how pressurised staff felt. A small error in the conversion of incoming information via telephone and teleprinter onto the map could lead to mistakes in the deployment of ships or aircraft with deadly consequences. She said that people were very conscious that the lives of sailors and merchant seamen depended on the accuracy of their work and the sometimes split-second decision making below ground in a Liverpool back street.

Working conditions were difficult. Former staff describe how people worked and slept underground for days at a time. Sun lamp radiation was

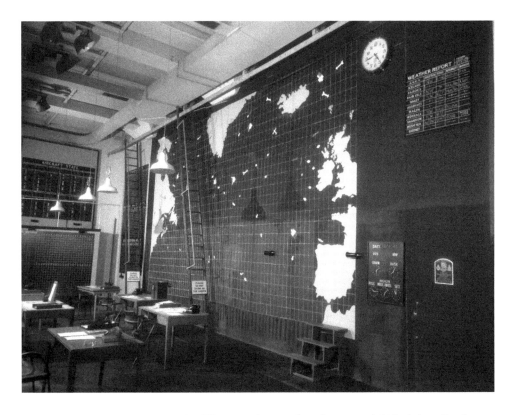

The operations room in the Western Approaches Command HQ below Derby House in Liverpool with the map showing the location of convoy ships, their protecting naval craft, as well as German U-boats. (Colin Philpott)

provided to try to compensate for the lack of sunlight experienced by people living in a bunker. However, the prevailing memory of many who worked there is the unpleasant smell which they describe as a mixture of sweat and cigarette smoke.

The deprivations of those in the bunker were as nothing compared with those engaged in the battle at sea: 2,603 British merchant ships and 175 naval vessels were sunk with the loss of an estimated 40,000 sailors, merchant seamen and others. Gradually, the Allies gained the upper hand and from 1943 onwards, the U-boat threat to Britain's supply lines was reduced, although never completely eliminated.

There is plenty of evidence that considerable precautions were taken to keep the location and true purpose of the bunker below Derby House a secret. There were five separate entrances to the complex above ground,

Plaque commemorating the role of Western Approaches Command headquarters constructed in Liverpool. There were five levels below ground, more than a hundred rooms and between 300 and 400 people worked there. (Colin Philpott)

which looked like office entrances. Indeed, some of them were also entrances to adjacent offices. Staff heading for the bunker were then able to access the bunker complex by a series of tunnels and staircases with heavily-guarded entrances. Once inside the complex, there were additional security points to prevent those without the highest security clearances from accessing the most sensitive parts of the command centre. As with many similar centres, there is no evidence that German intelligence knew the precise location of the Western Approaches Command bunker. However, historians have surmised that the Germans would have worked out that it was likely to be in Liverpool and may have tried to identify it but without success. It was never hit.

The Western Approaches Command was disbanded in August 1945, but the Liverpool bunker acquired a new role as a Royal Navy training centre until the 1960s. During this period, the veil of secrecy was maintained. This was a characteristic shared by many Second World War secret locations which were pressed into service during the Cold War. However, in the 1970s after the Ministry of Defence vacated the complex, its wartime role was first revealed. It opened as a museum in 1993 thanks to the efforts of a local architect Fred O'Brien who had campaigned for its preservation and public access. In 2017, the running of the museum was taken over by an organisation called Big Heritage.

Dover Castle, Kent

On the opposite side of the country and 250 miles to the south, another port played a major part in the British Second World War effort. However, the place at the centre of this effort was not a hastily constructed or converted building. Rather it was a medieval fortress which had already played an important role in the defence of Britain in earlier conflicts. It was to do so again in dramatic fashion between 1939 and 1945.

Dover Castle dates back at least to the eleventh century but its underground tunnels were first constructed during the Napoleonic Wars of the early nineteenth century. They were built as barracks to accommodate a garrison of more than 2,000 men. From 1826, the tunnels lay abandoned for more than a century. In 1939, however, the tunnels were once again pressed into service as an air-raid shelter and then as a command post. With its dominating view over the Straits of Dover, the castle was of prime strategic importance in the defence of Britain. The head of Dover Naval Command, Vice-Admiral Sir Bertram Ramsay, was given space in one of the tunnels to set up his headquarters.

Dover Castle, with its commanding position across the English Channel, has played a crucial role in the defence of Britain through the centuries including the Second World War. (Gael13011)

It was a role it had to perform rather sooner than anticipated. It was from there that the desperate evacuation of the Dunkirk beaches was directed, bringing back over 300,000 British and French troops at the end of May and beginning of June 1940. With British troops surrounded at Dunkirk on the French coast, Ramsay organised the famous flotilla of little ships that plucked the majority of the stranded troops from the beaches as they were strafed by Luftwaffe planes.

Later, other parts of the complex were used as a gun battery, a military hospital and once again as barracks. Then in 1942 and 1943 a new Command Headquarters (CHQ) was dug, below the level of the original 1939 Dunkirk command post, in preparation for the planned invasion of France by the Allies. When D-Day finally came in the summer of 1944, this CHQ was one of the places from which the invasion was masterminded. However, Dover's main role in the run-up to D-Day and at the time of the invasion itself was as a decoy. The D-Day deception (see Chapter Five) was successful at convincing the Germans that the invasion would happen at the narrowest part of the Channel landing in the Pas-de-Calais, rather than on the Normandy beaches.

During the first three years of the war secrecy was paramount at Dover. The underground complex was guarded both at the main gate to the castle and at the entrance to the tunnels. There is one report of a soldier who failed to produce identification being shot and injured at one of the security checkpoints. However, the castle complex was perhaps easier to guard and keep secret because Dover as a whole was quite difficult to enter. Throughout the war it was a highly regulated military area. The homes of most of the non-essential civilian population of the town were evacuated and the majority of the housing stock in Dover was given over to lodgings for the military. In that sense the Dover Castle tunnel complex was perhaps less vulnerable to leaks and infiltration than other sites of strategic significance in less obviously military locations.

In addition, like many other wartime locations which were to a greater or lesser extent secret, the principle of compartmentalisation came into play at Dover. Those working there were only allowed in the specific parts of the tunnels where they needed to be to do their jobs. So, people working in the military hospital would not have access to the CHQ. In this way, people did not see the whole story of what was happening at a particular secret facility. In this way the risk of leaks of information was reduced.

During the second half of the war, when the threat of invasion receded and the threat from the air reduced, there was a slightly more relaxed attitude to the Dover complex. According to the English Heritage Curator of Dover Castle, Rowena Willard-Wright, there was a propaganda value in using the iconic castle as a symbol of British fighting spirit and resilience, so a number of high-profile visits by Churchill and others were extensively publicised.

Although Dover Castle is highly visible, the underground complex was, of course, out of sight. Nevertheless, according to Willard-Wright, the Germans definitely knew of its existence and of its importance. They had flown reconnaissance aircraft over the castle prior to the war and are thought to have taken photographs of the diggings made in 1939. However, the complex was never directly targeted and only suffered minor damage caused by incendiary attacks.

After the war the tunnels were considered as one of the Regional Seats of Government in the event of nuclear attack during the Cold War.

Tunnels built into the coastline under Dover Castle housed commanders involved in the evacuation from Dunkirk and later the D-Day landings. This tunnel contains telephone signal repeater equipment. (Ian Taylor)

However, the tunnels were effectively closed by the Home Office despite being in the middle of a refit. British intelligence had identified Dover as a likely target for a Russian hydrogen bomb attack. Today, the whole site is managed by English Heritage and much of the tunnel complex is open to the public.

Special Operations Executive Bases

The role of the command centres discussed so far in this chapter was to direct the operations of the regular forces, but there were also scores of addresses across Britain during the Second World War from which secret operations behind enemy lines were launched. An innocuous-looking office block at **No.64 Baker Street, London** was the headquarters of the Special Operations Executive, a clandestine organisation designed to carry out espionage, sabotage and reconnaissance, first in German-occupied Europe and later also in Asia.

The story of the SoE remained secret for many years after the war but in more recent years has become a key part of the British Second World War narrative. It provides strong evidence of the idea that Britain and its Allies made very effective use of subterfuge, deception and dirty tricks to win the war. It has been the subject of many books and has provided story lines for more than a few films. However, most people are probably unaware of the size and scope of its operation which, at the peak of its activity, employed over 13,000 people, 5,000 of them agents in the field, and more than 3,000 of them women. Many of its agents were exiles from European countries occupied by the Nazis. Many died, some in concentration camps, because captured SoE agents were not, of course, regarded as prisoners of war.

The Special Operations Executive was the result of a reorganisation of clandestine operations by Winston Churchill after he became Prime Minister in May 1940. Previously, there had been several secret departments set up by different agencies of government. Churchill brought them together by creating the SoE in July 1940 and the Executive continued throughout the war directing sabotage operations behind enemy lines, including working with resistance organisations in France and elsewhere. The organisation was also involved in the establishment and direction of the auxiliary units, the British Resistance (see Chapter Six).

The man credited with turning the SoE into a formidable force was Major General Colin Gubbins, who was seconded to the Executive in November 1940 and later became its Director of Operations. SoE had many disputes and rows with other government departments and with the main armed services throughout the war. There were various attempts to disband or reorganise it. However, with the enthusiastic backing of the Prime Minister, it survived and made a major contribution to a whole range of special operations.

It had a number of objectives including fermenting civil disorder and resistance to force the Germans to devote more resources to maintaining order in occupied countries. It was also involved in a number of plans to assassinate key Nazis. These included the successful strike on Reinhard Heydrich in Prague in May 1942 and also plans to kill Hitler himself, never put into action. However, it also worked to build up resistance organisations and armed units that could and did help support Allied invaders after D-Day.

The administration of this network was centred on the area around Baker Street in Central London where a series of buildings were eventually used by the SoE. As well as No.64 Baker Street, other addresses in the area included **Norgeby House, 83 Baker Street; Montague Mansions, just off Baker Street; Michael House at No.82 Baker Street** (above the headquarters

The Special Operations Executive operated from several central London addresses including 64 Baker Street which became its headquarters from February 1940. (Richard Moss)

of Marks and Spencer); nearby **Bickenhall Mansions; Orchard Court in Portman Square,** where it is believed interviews with new recruits took place; and **1 Dorset Square,** where the Free French under General de Gaulle were based, and where a plaque now commemorates the building's wartime role. These premises were used partly as offices, partly for interviews and also as safe houses for agents. There was such a concentration of SoE activity in this area that the organisation enjoyed the soubriquet of the 'Baker Street Irregulars'.

The Special Operations Executive's bases were by no means confined to a small area of the capital. Although it is now impossible to know of every building used in some capacity or other by the organisation, there were more than sixty locations under the codename of STS (Special Training School). These were primarily used for training agents. In addition, there were a series of research and experimental stations used for developing equipment and weapons for use by SoE agents. There were also airfields specifically dedicated to SoE use. Many of these bases were in requisitioned country houses, many of them in the counties to the north of London. Indeed, the Executive occupied so many country houses that the joke at the time was that SoE really stood for 'Stately 'omes of England'.

Among the locations used by the SoE were:

The Frythe, Welwyn, Hertfordshire, known as Station IX, was a nineteenth-century country house requisitioned in August 1939 which became an important research and development centre for equipment and vehicles for SoE operations, including military vehicles, camouflage and other sabotage methods. After the war, it became a research base for Unilever and ICI and later for Glaxo Smith Kline. Since 2010 it has been redeveloped as luxury apartments.

Thatched Barn, Borehamwood, Hertfordshire was a mock Tudor hotel built in the 1930s which became a popular destination for film stars and others from the neighbouring Elstree Film Studios. It had been bought by the holiday camp pioneer, Billy Butlin, just prior to the war but was then requisitioned to become the SoE's Station XV, an important centre for the organisation's camouflage operation. Agents about to be sent behind enemy lines in France were kitted out with authentic French clothing. The Thatched Barn also developed a range of booby trap devices and other trick objects such as exploding bicycle pumps. After the war, it was derelict for a while, later briefly became a Playboy Club, then a hotel again until its demolition in the 1980s. A new hotel was built on the site in 1989.

Grendon Hall, near Grendon Underwood, Buckinghamshire, originally a private manor house built in the mid-nineteenth century, became a base for MI6 at the beginning of the war but was later a Signals Centre for SoE. It is now Spring Hill Open Prison.

THE FRYTHE

The Frythe, a country house in Hertfordshire known as Station IX, was requisitioned in August 1939 and became an important research and development centre for equipment and vehicles for the Special Operations Executive. (Unknown)

Arisaig House, near Lochaber, Inverness-shire was an important centre for paramilitary training for SoE agents. Hundreds were trained there including many Czech and Slovak exiles. A memorial in their memory was unveiled at the site in 2009.

Beaulieu House, Beaulieu, Hampshire. The famous south coast stately home was another training centre for agents who learned a range of sabotage and deception techniques there including burglary, forgery and the use of special devices like lethal blades hidden in shoelaces.

RAF Tangmere, near Chichester, West Sussex had been an RAF airfield since the First World War. During the Second World War it was a base for Spitfires and operated as a regular airfield. It was severely bombed with the loss of twenty lives on 16 August 1940 during the Battle of Britain. However, it had a double life as a secret airfield for the SoE which used it as a base for flying its agents into France. Tangmere was vacated by the RAF in 1970 and much of the land returned to farming, but there is a museum there commemorating its wartime role.

Yet another country house, this one near Lochaber in the north of Scotland, was involved in Special Operations Executive training. Arisaig House was used for paramilitary training. (Arisaig House)

RAF Harrington, near Kettering, Northamptonshire operated as a US Air Force base from 1943 and was the base for Operation Carpetbagger, the supplying of weapons and materials to resistance fighters in occupied Europe in advance of the D-Day landings. The operation, which began in January 1944, used specially adapted B-24 Liberator bombers that flew to drop points in France and elsewhere. After dropping their cargos, the pilots often flew some distance further in order to try to disguise the drop points. In July 1944 alone, Carpetbagger missions delivered over 5,000 containers, 3,000 packages, more than 1,500 bundles of leaflets as well as sixty-nine agents and seven pigeons! There is now a museum on the site of the airfield.

Other Command Centres

There were scores of other important command centres for the Army, Navy, RAF and other services during the Second World War including:
Bunker 13, Kenton, Newcastle-Upon-Tyne

Beneath modern residential streets on the edge of Newcastle lies another RAF Operations Room which thousands of people will pass close by every day without realising. No.13 Group Operations Room was built beneath the Kenton district of Newcastle, to the same design as the Uxbridge bunker, and was put into service on 3 December 1939. It was the HQ for the group which covered the North of England, Scotland and Northern Ireland. The site was known as RAF Blakelaw and there were three parts to the complex. The Operations Room, which is below Ashover Road, and was accessed from an innocuous-looking surface building, was the epicentre of the operation. On the other side of what is now the A167, there was a filter room – where incoming information was handled. There was also a communications room, but its location is now unknown.

Although the main focus of the Battle of Britain was over the south-east, there was significant activity over the area covered by No.13 Group from Newcastle. As well as intercepting Luftwaffe attacks on its own area, No.13 Group also lent squadrons to other groups to defend the Midlands and southern England during the Battle of Britain. Testimony from those who

Inside the No.13 Group Operations Room below Newcastle which the Bunker 13 Group hopes to reopen for private tours and school trips. (Colin Anderson)

worked there suggests that secrecy was taken very seriously. WAAFs who worked there were escorted from the guarded entrance to the rooms where they worked and not allowed to walk around other parts of the underground complex.

After the end of the war, the facilities at Kenton were variously used as a Regional War Room for the north-east during the early years of the Cold War, as a training centre and as storage for various government offices later built above ground on parts of the RAF Blakelaw site.

Today, the operations room is a Grade Two listed building and when developers built housing on the site, it was a planning condition that the bunker remains accessible. In 2009 a preservation group was set up to try to raise money to reopen the bunker for school visits and private tours. As of 2018, this had not yet been achieved. As the site is in the middle of a residential area, there are no plans to make it open to the general public.

The surface level building in Ashover Road in the Kenton area of Newcastle, now in the middle of modern housing estate, which was the access to the No.13 Group Operations Room of RAF Fighter Command during the war. (Colin Anderson)

RAF Fighter Command, Bentley Priory, Stanmore, London

Bentley Priory was the overall headquarters of RAF Fighter Command and it was where Hugh Dowding based himself throughout his time as commander. The Group Operations Rooms all reported into Bentley Priory. Originally built in 1766, the priory was acquired by the RAF in 1926 but became Fighter Command's HQ in 1936. Its operations room was originally above ground but a new one was built about 15 metres below ground and opened in March 1940. King George VI, Winston Churchill and the US General Dwight D. Eisenhower monitored the D-Day landings from the bunker at Bentley Priory. The Germans were aware of Bentley Priory as two senior Luftwaffe officers were entertained there in 1938. However, there is no evidence of the Priory having ever been the intended target of a bombing raid. A few bombs, believed to be intended for central London, did land there causing only very minor damage.

After the war, the priory remained an important RAF centre but the buildings deteriorated and suffered two major fires. In 2008 the RAF vacated the site. A museum now occupies part of the site, but the bunker has been filled in.

RAF Rudloe Manor, Near Corsham, Wiltshire

Known during the Second World War as RAF Box, named after the settlement of Box near Corsham, this was the headquarters of No.10 Group of Fighter Command covering the south-west of England and South Wales. The operations room, filter room and communications room were all located in Brown's Quarry, part of the vast underground wartime facility below Corsham. The RAF station closed in 2000 but the site retains a military role.

RAF Bomber Command, High Wycombe, Buckinghamshire

After the reorganisation of the RAF in 1936, a location was needed for the Bomber Command division and a site at Walters Ash near High Wycombe was chosen. Like many of the crucial defence establishments of the Second World War, places in the northern Home Counties were often favoured. They were relatively close to London but were on the 'right' side of the capital in that they were thought to be less vulnerable to German bombing. Much effort was expended to keep Bomber Command HQ secret. Many of its buildings were disguised by making them look like other things – the fire station like a church and the officers' mess like a manor house. The plentiful tree cover of the area was maintained as far as possible. The main operations room was built 15 metres below ground. The complex was named Southdown and its postal address was GPO (General Post Office) High Wycombe. In 2018, RAF High Wycombe remains operational.

Hughenden Manor, near High Wycombe, Buckinghamshire

Known as Operation Hillside, Britain's top-secret cartography operation was based at the stately home of Hughenden Manor near High Wycombe, close to RAF Bomber Command. From 1941 until 1945 it produced detailed maps of bombing target areas for use by the RAF. These included maps for the Dambusters Raid and also for D-Day. The creation of this operation in 1941 was ordered in response to what was considered to be a serious lack of accurate maps of Germany held by the Allies. Germany had stopped the commercial production of maps some years before the war so maps initially available to the RAF were somewhat out of date. In large part the maps needed for use by RAF Bomber Command had to be made from aerial photographs taken by reconnaissance planes once the war was underway.

More than a hundred people worked at Hughenden and they say the operation was highly secret because the cartographers were effectively armed with knowledge of the RAF's planned bombing targets. However, there was no obvious heavy security around the site and this was yet another example of a crucial location 'hidden in plain sight' by deliberately not drawing attention to it. The story of Hughenden was one of the last to be revealed and remained secret until almost sixty years after the war. It came to light when visitors to the stately home, run by the National Trust, were overheard talking about their wartime experiences there.

RAF Coastal Command, Northwood, Hertfordshire

The RAF took over Eastbury Park at Northwood in 1939 and established a headquarters for its Coastal Command in Eastbury House and in a number of underground facilities specially built at the time. It is now Northwood Headquarters and, arguably, the most important military establishment in Britain. It houses several operational commands including joint commands of Britain's armed services as well as hosting a number of multi-national defence bodies. Several recent wars, including the Falklands, Iraq and Afghanistan, have been directed from here.

Known as Operation Hillside, Britain's top-secret cartography operation was based at Hughenden Manor near High Wycombe. It produced target maps for RAF bombing operations including the Dambusters Raid. (Giacomo)

Fort Southwick, Portsmouth, Hampshire

An underground complex of tunnels was excavated at Fort Southwick on the hills above Portsmouth to create a naval command base for the expected invasion of mainland Europe. The excavation was done by the Royal Engineers between February and December 1942 to create an underground communications and control hub buried 30 metres below ground. A secure underground radio station was also built in the nearby Paulsgrove Chalk Pit. Although D-Day planning took place elsewhere, Portsmouth became the operational basis for the Allied commanders once the invasion was imminent. The American Supreme Commander of the Allied Expeditionary Force, General Dwight D. Eisenhower, the British Commander, General Sir Bernard Montgomery and the Naval Commander, Admiral Sir Bertram Ramsay based themselves at nearby

Southwick House, although the functional headquarters were hidden in tents in nearby woods. The underground tunnels of Fort Southwick were relinquished by the Ministry of Defence in 2003. A private company now uses some of the underground complex as a centre for mock battle games.

Portland Naval Base, Portland, Dorset

A similar excavation project took place in the hillside above Portland Harbour. Two tunnels were cut into the hills leading to a network of rooms buried underground. The complex, completed in 1941, operated as a sub-command base for Fort Southwick in Portsmouth. It contained a naval operations room and associated facilities. After the war, the base had occasional use in the Cold War but was abandoned in the 1960s.

Camp Griffiss, Bushy Park, London

Camp Griffiss was created from scratch in the grounds of Bushy Park in 1942 as the European base for the US Air Force. Housed in temporary buildings in one section of the park, the camp was named after Lieutenant Colonel Townsend Griffiss who was the first American killed when the United States entered the war. It performed several roles but most importantly was used by Eisenhower as the main base for planning Operation Overlord – the D-Day landings. Camp Griffiss continued to be used by the US Air Force and the RAF after the war but the temporary buildings were removed by the 1960s. There are two memorials commemorating Camp Griffiss in Bushy Park.

Wentworth Estate Bunker, Virginia Water, Surrey

The Wentworth Estate at Virginia Water, including the Wentworth Golf Course, was requisitioned at the beginning of the war for military uses. A series of tunnels were dug in front of the golf pavilion and an underground complex was created as an unspecified emergency refuge in case of the need to evacuate key military command facilities from central London. In the end it was used first as headquarters for the Home Forces. From 1943 they vacated Wentworth which then became one of the HQs for Supreme Headquarters Allied Expeditionary Forces. Once D-Day was imminent, Wentworth became a rear HQ providing supply and administration for

A memorial commemorating Camp Griffiss which was built in Bushy Park in London to provide a European base for the US Airforce. It was named after Lieutenant Colonel Townsend Griffiss who was the first American killed when the United States entered the war. (Jonathan Cardy)

Operation Overlord. After the war the tunnels were handed back to the golf club and have since been sealed.

Churchill's War Room, Whitehall, London

No account of British Second World War secret command centres would be complete without mention of the most iconic of them all, the Cabinet War Rooms, more popularly known now as Churchill's War Room, which was effectively the epicentre of the command and control structure of the entire British war effort. Arguably the most important of all wartime locations, it was the place where crucial discussions took place between members of the War Cabinet and the Chiefs of Staff. It was the space in which key military decisions were taken which determined the course of the war.

In the 2017 film *Darkest Hour* Churchill's private secretary Elizabeth Layton, played by Lily James, arrives for her first day of work in the War Rooms. As she is rushed through the warren of tunnels to start work with the Prime Minister, she is told never to speak to anyone about what she does there or what she sees or hears. This appears to be the sum total of the security briefing for a new member of the team working below ground at the very heart of Britain's war command. Even though this is clearly dramatic licence, it is probably not far from the truth of what actually happened. Elizabeth Layton would have been required to sign the Official Secrets Act. However, at the War Rooms, as at many other similarly sensitive places, much reliance appears to have been put on faith in the sense of duty of people working there.

The epicentre of the British war command structure, the Cabinet War Rooms below Whitehall were ready for use on 27 August 1939, just days before Britain declared war on Germany. (Imperial War Museum)

Ilene Hutchinson worked as a shorthand typist in the Cabinet War Rooms and remembered how tight the security was:

> 'Security was very tough. Entering the building we had to sign on at the times we were scheduled to sign on. We had a Marine just on the left of us as we were going down. He was like a waxwork in Madame Tussaud's just standing there with his rifle at the ready and his red-banded hat and not fluttering an eyebrow.'

The Cabinet War Rooms had been opened on 27 August 1939 just a week before Britain declared war on Germany. Their construction was first discussed in 1937. Originally, the plan had been to evacuate key government personnel to the suburbs of London or even further from London, possibly to the West Country. However, this idea was abandoned because of fears that the Government leaving London would be damaging to public morale during wartime. The German invasion of Austria in March 1938 brought an added sense of urgency to the search that was by then underway for a suitable war room in London. Given the possibility of war starting suddenly during the spring of 1938, the search turned to suitable basements in existing buildings. On 31 May 1938, it was confirmed that the best option was to convert the basement of what was known as the New Public Offices, close to Downing Street and to Parliament.

Under the direction of General Hastings Ismay, Deputy Secretary of Britain's Committee of Imperial Defence, the basement was transformed with brick partitions built, alcoves sandbagged, and air locks and steel doors fitted to protect against gas attacks. Telephone lines were installed and the BBC created a broadcasting link to the bunker. The centrepiece was the map room where vital military intelligence was displayed. There was a separate main meeting room used by the War Cabinet. A ventilation system was added in a week in September 1938 and by the end of that month, the War Rooms were ready in case of emergency. The Munich Agreement, signed on 30 September, which the then Prime Minister, Neville Chamberlain wrongly believed offered 'peace in our time' did at least afford extra time for war preparations. As far as the War Rooms were concerned, this allowed time to make the working and living conditions below ground more tolerable. Dormitories and chemical toilets were added and the ventilation system improved.

During the 'phoney war' period from September 1939 until May 1940, the expected aerial bombardment did not materialise. The War Cabinet first met in the underground war rooms in October 1939 but just to test the facilities. However, once the Battle of Britain was underway and after Churchill replaced Chamberlain as Prime Minister, the new facility came into its own. Extra staff were drafted in, new communications facilities were added and rooms were sub-divided to create extra space. It was cramped and claustrophobic, but it was from here, with the threat of invasion real in the summer of 1940, that the defence of Britain was led.

Staff working there at the beginning of the war believed they were safe from bombing or chemical attack. However, in September 1940, it was discovered that the War Rooms would not be protected in the event of a direct hit on the building above. A thick concrete slab was added and an extra exterior wall put up at ground level to reduce the vulnerability of the War Rooms from a direct hit.

The War Cabinet met below ground in the Cabinet War Rooms 115 times between October 1939 and March 1945 and the complex provided living quarters for Britain's top politicians and military commanders. (Imperial War Museum)

From 1940 onwards until August 1945, the Cabinet War Rooms were operational twenty-four hours a day. Churchill didn't like sleeping there, although he did have a bedroom and spent the night there sometimes. He and his wife spent more nights in the No.10 Annexe which was created for them in the building above. However, it was underground that the daily business of directing the war took place. It was there that Britain's most senior military figures, intelligence chiefs and most senior politicians lived and worked cheek by jowl throughout the conflict. Churchill used the BBC studio there to broadcast to the nation on several occasions. A transatlantic phone link was installed in 1943 which enabled Churchill to talk to the US President. When the War Cabinet met there on 28 March 1945 for the final time, it was the 115th time it had done so.

The Cabinet War Rooms escaped damage from bombing or later in the war from rocket attacks. The closest hit was in September 1940 when a bomb landed near the present-day entrance to the War Rooms. There is no evidence that the security of this vital nerve centre was ever compromised.

Like many vital wartime locations, there were in fact two back-up facilities in place. Had the Whitehall centre been taken out of commission, the War Cabinet and Chiefs of Staff could have moved to an alternative facility in the suburbs of north London known as the Paddock (see Chapter Six). However, another alternative Cabinet War Room was also developed underneath Whitehall. Known by the codename 'Anson', it was created in 1943 in an underground complex known as the Rotundas in the Marsham Street area. It was completed in November 1943 although it never had to be used. Other parts of the Rotundas complex were used during and after the war by various government agencies. The current Home Office building now stands on the site.

Meanwhile, the lights in the Cabinet War Rooms themselves were turned off on 16 August 1945, the day after Japan's surrender had brought the Second World War to an end. Many of the rooms were cleared. Some were re-purposed for general government use. However, the main rooms of historical significance were left undisturbed and were declared a monument in 1948. Free guided tours were available on request right up to the 1980s when the Imperial War Museum was asked to take charge of the site and turn it into a museum with public access. The museum opened in 1984 and it is now one of the most popular tourist attractions in Britain.

Overall Assessment

The security and secrecy of the command centres featured (and of many others) was achieved by a number of means. All were guarded by so-called Blue Cap military police, the unit with a particular responsibility for vulnerable locations. Many, like the Cabinet War Rooms and the Battle of Britain Command, were in specially-built underground bunkers whose surface entrances were well concealed. Others were effectively 'hidden in plain sight', so housed in country homes which would look very much as they did in peacetime from the air, or indeed disguised in or below ordinary urban buildings, like the Western Approaches Command in Liverpool.

Nearly everyone working in these command centres was service personnel and apparently accepted, largely without question, that they were engaged in secret work about which they should keep quiet. And, finally, the compartmentalisation principle seemed to apply in all cases. People were only told what they needed to know to do their particular job which reduced the chances of leakages of information.

Chapter Three

Spying and Listening Bases

Bletchley Park; the 'other' Bletchley Parks; 'Y' Listening stations;
Chain Home Radar; the Royal Observer Corps

Bletchley Park, Buckinghamshire

Gwen Adsley's parents died in 1966 without ever knowing that their daughter had worked at Bletchley Park. Gwen Hook, as she then was, started at the code-breaking centre in Buckinghamshire in the autumn of 1942 and worked there until October 1944. She has a very strong memory of her arrival at the Park after travelling by train from London.

> 'The first thing we had to do was to sign the Official Secrets Act. Then the man in charge told us in no uncertain terms that the most important thing was secrecy. He told us that we were never to talk about what we did, not outside of the hut where we worked, not in the canteen and certainly not outside the Park, even to family and friends and not even after the war ended.'

Gwen's work was laborious and repetitive. She worked in a hut with the windows boarded up and no natural daylight on a three-shift system, including overnights. Her job was to transcribe the coded messages. Gwen explained:

> 'Work came through the pneumatic tubes which ran down the walls into a basket next to Betty; she was the senior, in charge of us, and was a bit older than we were. She took out the tubes, unscrewed the ends and took out the sheets. There were groups of five letters across the page and first of all you altered the groups by drawing a line down the first two letters then redid them. Then you took the first group which was, say, AFGKL, and you wrote a particular new letter under each original letter in pencil. It always remained the same, so you got to know very quickly what each letter was.'

Gwen Adsley, who worked at Bletchley Park from 1942 until 1944, transcribing coded messages, never told her parents about the work she had done during the war. (Bletchley Park Trust)

Gwen, now in her nineties, told me in 2018 how she obeyed the instruction explicitly.

'I kept to it very strictly. When I went home on leave to see my parents, they never pressed me on exactly what I did. If they asked me about it, I just said that I was doing boring old office work. I feel sad now that I didn't ever tell them after the war. My dad would have been very proud.'

Gwen's experience and the story of Bletchley Park go right to the heart of the matter of secrecy in Second World War Britain. The work done there to break German, Italian and Japanese codes is now deemed to have been one of the most significant factors in determining the outcome of the war in the Allies' favour. Although Germany also broke some Allied codes, they were less significant breaches of security than those they suffered at the hands of the British and American codebreakers. In addition, Germany had several, often competing, intelligence agencies who failed to pool and share information in the way the Allies did. This crucial advantage is often said to have shortened the war by at least two years.

The Bletchley story also epitomises some key characteristics of the secrecy surrounding the most sensitive locations in Britain during the war. David Kenyon, the resident historian at Bletchley Park, maintains that the Germans never discovered that Bletchley was the centre of the British codebreaking operation. Certainly, it appears never to have been deliberately targeted by German bombers. One bomb landed in the grounds in November 1940, but the nearby railway station is believed to have been the target. Interviews with German intelligence officers after the war confirmed that the Nazis had never identified the site's importance.

What's more, the role played by Bletchley Park during the war remained unknown to the general public for thirty years after the end of the conflict. Even after the first public discussion about Bletchley in the 1970s, many of those who had worked there were still reluctant to talk about it. All these facts can now, with the benefit of hindsight, seem remarkable. To understand them, we need to go back to the origins of Bletchley Park and to the way its operations were organised.

The Bletchley Park mansion and grounds were bought by the then head of the Secret Intelligence Service (SIS), Admiral Sir Hugh Sinclair, in 1938 as a suitable relocation of his organisation and of the Government Code and Cypher School (GC&CS) in the event of war. The choice of location was deliberate. It was right next to Bletchley Railway Station on the West Coast main line route, but also on the Varsity Line linking Oxford and Cambridge. It was expected that many of those chosen to work there would be recruited from Oxbridge. It was also near what was then the main road to London and it was close to important communications links routed through nearby

Throughout the war 11,000 people worked at Bletchley Park in more than twenty different buildings, and their codebreaking is estimated to have shortened the conflict by at least two years. (GCHQ)

Fenny Stratford. In addition, like many of the locations chosen for important wartime work, it was on the northern side of London, perceived to be less vulnerable to bombing than the southern Home Counties, but still easily accessible from the capital.

In the period before war was declared, the codebreaking capacity of the new centre was built up with existing code experts transferred from GC&CS in London and by recruiting academic high-flyers mainly from Oxford and Cambridge universities. These included talented mathematicians mostly recruited through personal contacts. Administrative and clerical staff needed to support them were initially also found through personal contacts and usually from what was described at the time as the 'upper echelons' of society.

Over the next six years, Bletchley Park undertook a range of codebreaking activities. The best-known was the breaking of the Enigma codes used by the German military. In fact, it was Polish codebreakers who had first cracked Enigma and shared their intelligence with the British and French just before the war began. The Bletchley Park codebreakers developed the electromechanical machines known as 'bombes' which were used to identify the daily settings of the German Enigma codes. This technology, developed particularly by the celebrated Cambridge mathematician, Alan Turing, was the key to breaking Enigma. It was a process that was helped by the capture of German codebooks and a certain lack of discipline in the way the Germans used the codes.

The bombes were first used to break Luftwaffe codes and later German naval codes. Later in the war, the Colossus machine, effectively the world's first digital computer, was developed by Tommy Flowers at the Post Office Research Station in North London and that was brought into use at Bletchley Park in time for D-Day. This speeded up the codebreaking process considerably. In total, it is estimated that throughout the course of the war the operation at Bletchley intercepted more than 2.5million enemy messages.

The codebreaking achievements of Bletchley Park gave the Allies crucial strategic forewarning of German, Japanese and other Axis powers' plans in relation to many key battles and operations. These included Luftwaffe bombing raids, U-boat positions during the Battle of the Atlantic, decisive intelligence during the North African campaign and the pinpointing of the location of virtually every German division defending the French coast at the time of the D-Day landings.

So how was the secrecy of such a key intelligence operation maintained? Throughout the war, a total of more than 11,000 people worked at Bletchley Park and at its peak, in January 1945, there were 8,995 at one time. Given the numbers of people involved, it is perhaps unsurprising that there were security breaches. The most notorious was that involving John Cairncross, who many years after the war was exposed as the 'Fifth Man' in the so-called Cambridge spy-ring. Cairncross, already working as a Soviet spy when war broke out, managed to get himself posted to Bletchley and leaked intelligence gained there to the Russians. Although Britain and the Soviet Union were Allies from 1941 onwards, Churchill did not share the full story of Bletchley's exploits with Moscow. The British did not want the Russians to know how they had obtained information. However, Cairncross provided a range of material to the Soviets, including details about the atomic weapons research being undertaken by Britain and the United States.

There were also a number of much lower level security breaches – mainly people who were overheard talking about their work outside

Passport photograph of Alan Turing aged 16. Turing was the most famous of the Bletchley Park codebreakers. (Unknown)

of Bletchley. There were a few instances of people disappearing from Bletchley mysteriously, believed to have been spirited away after they had been identified as security risks. More often, though, anyone who was suspected of careless, rather than deliberate, breaches received a visit from

A demonstration of how the bombe codebreaking machines worked using a reconstruction now in place at Bletchley Park. The bombes were used to break Luftwaffe and later German naval codes. (Colin Philpott)

an Intelligence Officer and was subjected to a 'friendly chat' designed to put the 'frighteners' on them.

The security of Bletchley Park was fundamentally achieved by two means – physical security but more importantly social and emotional pressure. It was guarded by military police and everyone working there needed a pass to get in. If a member of staff forgot their pass, they wouldn't be admitted. Crucially, the physical layout and organisation of the site helped reduce the risk of leaks of information. There were more than twenty different buildings, including the famous huts where different aspects of the work were carried on. Everything was very compartmentalised and people were only allowed access to their working area. When using the canteen and other shared facilities, staff were under strict instructions not to discuss their particular work, so few people had the overall picture of what was happening there. However, no particular attempt was made to conceal the site and, to the outside world, it will have looked very much like yet another English country estate. It was the example, par excellence, of something 'hidden in plain sight'.

Interestingly, rumours were put about during 1938 and 1939, when the estate was being prepared for its wartime role, that it was to be a centre for air defence training. Later, there was a local belief that it was some sort of hospital for service people, perhaps for those with mental illness brought on by the horrors of war. This belief was perhaps fuelled by witnessing what some local people thought was unusual and eccentric behaviour by some Bletchley staff when they were out and about near the Park.

However, the secrecy depended less on physical security and more on a combination of personal trust, contemporary attitudes and social pressure. None of the Bletchley staff lived on the estate; all were billeted with local families. All were allowed leave – in most cases four weeks a year and there was no policing of where people went when they were off–duty. None of the veterans I have spoken to recalls any searching of bags when people left the site.

Bletchley staff were even encouraged to get involved in social activities outside the Park. With a high proportion of Bletchley's staff being young, university-educated (unusual at the time) and interested in arts and culture, a whole host of cultural and leisure activities were organised on the site. But later in the war, Bletchley staff mixed with local people, particularly at Wilton Hall which was built just outside what was then the main entrance to the Park in Wilton Avenue. Wilton Hall, which is still in use today, was an entertainment venue for concerts, dances and other events which was used by both Bletchley Park staff and the local population.

People were, it appears, trusted to keep quiet about what they did. David Kenyon, Bletchley's historian, ascribes this to a number of factors. There was a much stronger sense of deference to authority than exists in the twenty-first century. Most people were prepared to accept that the war had to be won and that they would put up with things and not ask awkward questions. This was an attitude that would have pervaded the vast majority of people during the war. So, keeping quiet about sensitive information was necessary for service personnel on the front line, for people working in munitions factories just as much as for people working in codebreaking. In a sense, there was nothing remarkable about it at the time.

Bletchley Park and its grounds had been purchased by the then head of the Secret Intelligence Service (SIS), Admiral Sir Hugh Sinclair, in 1938 as a suitable relocation of his organisation and of the Government Code and Cypher School (GC&CS) in the event of war. (Colin Philpott)

There was also a fear of the consequences of letting slip information – fear of possible prosecution under the Official Secrets Act, a fear that breaches of security could endanger the lives of loved ones and people at the front and a fear that information leaks could directly damage the war effort.

A note issued to all Bletchley Park staff in May 1942 warned against the dangers of 'Careless Talk':

Secrecy – this may seem a simple matter. It should be. But repeated experience has proved that it is not, even for the cleverest of us; even for the least important. Month after month instances have occurred where workers at BP have been heard casually saying things outside BP that are dangerous. It is not enough to know that you must not hint at these things outside. It must be uppermost in your mind every hour that you talk to outsiders. Even the most trivial-seeming things matter. The enemy does not get his intelligence by great scoops, but from a whisper here, a tiny detail there.

The note went on to instruct staff not to talk at meals, not to talk in the transport, or when travelling, or in the billet, or by their own fireside and even to be careful in their own hut. The note concluded with this stark warning:

There is nothing to be gained by chatter but the satisfaction of idle vanity, or idle curiosity: there is everything to be lost – the very existence of our work here, the lives of others, even the war itself.

There was also a strong desire to avoid ending up with a feeling of shame by being the person who'd 'blabbed' about the crucial work that was being undertaken there. It is believed that some people delayed or avoided necessary medical operations because they feared what they might say if under the effects of anaesthetic!

In addition, David Kenyon believes that Bletchley's staff, both the intellectual heavyweights and the administrative and clerical staff who supported them, came from quite a narrow strata of society. They were overwhelmingly middle-class, mostly upper middle-class and they were therefore much more likely, in line with the cultural mores of the time, to safeguard the secrecy of what they were doing.

There was one other crucial factor which helped maintain secrecy. Only in the most exceptional circumstances were staff at Bletchley Park allowed to leave their jobs there. They were considered in many cases to have too much knowledge to risk them falling into enemy hands if, for example, they were allowed to join the armed forces and fight on the front line.

From August 1945, when the war finally ended with the surrender of Japan, the Bletchley Park operation was wound down fairly quickly. In June 1946, GC&CS, renamed GCHQ (Government Communications Headquarters) was moved to Eastcote in North London and later to Cheltenham where it remains to this day. Two of the Colossus computers and fifty of the bombes were taken to Eastcote but the rest were destroyed. Some Bletchley staff stayed with the organisation but most were either made redundant or moved elsewhere into other government jobs. They were made to sign the Official Secrets Act again when they left their jobs.

Work in the Bletchley Park huts was highly compartmentalised and people gen-erally were only aware of what was happening in the hut where they worked. (Colin Philpott)

Perhaps what is even more remarkable than the secrecy which was maintained around Bletchley Park during the war is the fact that its role remained a secret for a further thirty years. There are two main reasons for this. Firstly, the expertise and technology which had made it such a success in the war were still very much needed by the British military and intelligence communities after 1945. Germany, Italy and Japan were no longer the enemy but the Soviet Union and its eastern European satellites. British codebreaking capacity was now turned towards a new target and it was therefore important that the secrets of Bletchley Park remained hidden.

The second reason was to do with the attitude of the people who had worked there. Most Bletchley Park veterans took their signing of the Official Secrets Act very seriously and understood that it was for life. The habit of keeping quiet about it, instilled in them during the war, just carried on. Also, like everyone else, after nearly six years of war, they were keen to get on with their lives. Bletchley's staff were mainly young people who had sacrificed some of the best years of their lives working long hours in fairly grim working conditions on monotonous and often very repetitive and mind-numbing work. Looking back from the twenty-first century, it is very easy to see the Bletchley Park veterans as having been engaged in heroic, glamorous, ground-breaking work. Indeed they were, but it would not have seemed like that to many of them at the time. In addition, it was quite common for people not to talk about what they had done in the war. Many people who had served on the front line did not wish to relive the horrors they had seen. In this context, it was easier for Bletchley's codebreakers to keep quiet.

The first substantial revelation of the wartime role of Bletchley Park came with the publication of F.W. Winterbotham's book *The Ultra Secret* in 1974 and thereafter public awareness grew. The Bletchley Park site itself went through a number of post-war uses including as a training college for teachers, for the Civil Aviation Authority, the Post Office, BT and GCHQ. By the 1990s, much of the site was derelict and in danger of redevelopment. In 1992, the site was declared a conservation area and a trust was formed to preserve it. In 1994 visitors were first allowed onto the site and subsequently it has been developed into a museum which now attracts over 250,000 visitors a year.

It was only in 2009 that the Ministry of Defence told Bletchley Park veterans that they were no longer bound by the Official Secrets Act in relation to their work there. More than 1,000 are still known to be alive in 2018 and the Bletchley Park Trust organises annual reunions for them. The vast majority are pleased that their wartime work, for so long a secret, has now been given public recognition. Even now, though, some of the veterans have a few regrets about the publicity.

Gwen Adsley has only been back to Bletchley Park once since she left there in 1944 and even now doesn't often talk about her time there. She says:

> 'I was a bit upset when the story came out. I had vowed not to talk about it. But I can see that the younger generation need to know about it. I was very happy when I worked there. I enjoyed the company of the other girls and I liked the countryside. But you can't recreate that feeling after all these years.'

The 'Other Bletchleys' – Bletchley Park's Out-stations

Another means of protecting the vital work of Bletchley Park was to spread its activities to other sites. As with many other wartime installations, the principle of dispersal applied to codebreaking, so there was more than one Bletchley Park. There were in fact five other sites, three of them quite close to Bletchley Park, where codebreakers worked during the Second World War. These sites were controlled by Bletchley Park but, by the end of the war, around 200 bombes were located at the out-stations and only nine at Bletchley itself. Bletchley's historian, David Kenyon, says this is a crucial and often overlooked aspect of the codebreakers' story. Although great effort was put into maintaining the secrecy of the Park and protecting it, a bombing raid there would not have disabled Britain's codebreaking capacity.

Ruth Bourne – Ruth Henry as she then was – worked as a bombe operator and checker at two of the out-stations, Eastcote and Stanmore, both in North-West London between August 1943 and December 1945. She recalls the working and living conditions at Eastcote.

> 'Block A was where we lived, ate and slept. There were seventy-two of us in the barracks. It was revolting with double bunks and very flimsy curtains which made it difficult to sleep during the day when you were on night-duty. The food was appalling but at least it was hot.
>
> Block B was where we worked. We swapped roles. One day I would be plugging up the 'bombe' and the next shift I would be checking my 'oppo's' work. If you got a good 'stop', you would pick up the red scrambler phone and report to the person at the other end, who I now know was at Bletchley Park. I had no idea

Derelict buildings at Eastcote which was one of five out-stations for the Bletchley Park codebreaking operation. One hundred bombes were located here and over 800 Wrens worked there. (Unknown)

exactly what it all meant but I knew it was good if we got a match on the codes. We used codenames to indicate a match so that, if anyone had hacked into the phones, they wouldn't know what we were talking about it.'

Ruth told me that she obviously knew they were involved in codebreaking but that she didn't understand how her particular work fitted into the overall operation and that, at the time, she was unaware of Enigma or any of the other details of the bigger picture. 'We knew nothing. We never knew if the work had contributed to military success. It was a bit like doing your homework but never getting it marked,' she said.

Ruth remembers the security at Eastcote. There were high walls, barbed wire, armed guards and most of the windows were virtually blacked out:

'We worked, ate and slept and stayed on the site most of the time. If we left the site, we needed to show our ID to get back in, but I don't remember any searches when we went out. If you forgot or lost your pass, you got a stiff reprimand. If it happened a second time, I believe people had money docked from their wages.'

Ruth and her colleagues had to sign the Official Secrets Act and she told me that there was no question in her mind at the time that she would have discussed her work with anyone, even her own family. Her family never asked her the details of what she was doing. If they had, she maintains she would not have told them. She puts this down to two factors, firstly, she had an absolute commitment to the war effort.

'All I knew at the time was that anything I was doing to help kill Germans was worth doing. It sounds awful to me now but that's how it was at the time. Anything we could do to get rid of Hitler was worthwhile. We were incredibly naïve then but that's what we thought.'

Secondly, Ruth also believes that the maintenance of the secrecy of the codebreaking operation was very much down to the social attitudes and assumptions of the sort of people who were chosen to work at Bletchley and its out-stations. She told me:

'The overwhelming majority of people who worked as codebreakers were from middle or upper-class upbringings. They had been told from an early age that they must do as they were told for the common good. People were imbued with a sense of country and duty. That's probably why we kept quiet.'

Ruth also believes that the sanction of prison for breaking the Official Secrets Act or other punishment was quite a deterrent. 'People from my sort of background never went to prison. The shame would have been too great.'
      There were five Bletchley out-stations:

Eastcote. The out-station at Eastcote, in what is now the London Borough of Hillingdon, was developed on a site that had been commandeered originally for use as a military hospital to take casualties from the D-Day landings. However, it was not needed for this and an out-station was established there. 'HMS *Pembroke*' was the code name cover used for the deployment of Wrens to Eastcote and other codebreaking stations. Eastcote had 100 bombe machines, operated by 800 Wrens and 100 RAF technicians. The Americans also had use of part of the site for their own bombes. After the war, Eastcote became the centre of the government's codebreaking operations with the closure of Bletchley Park until the move to new purpose-built headquarters in Cheltenham. The Eastcote site remained in various government uses until 2009 since when it has been redeveloped for housing.

Gayhurst House is a sixteenth century manor house which became an out-station for Bletchley Park in September 1942. At least five bombes were located there in temporary huts built in the grounds. More than 200 people were stationed there, some billeted in the house and some in huts. Glen Miller's band is understood to have entertained staff there during the war.

Anne Lewis-Smith joined the WRNS and recalled her interview before being posted to Gayhurst: 'If you accept this posting, you will never be able to talk about it for the rest of your life. Will you agree to that? I agreed and I signed the Official Secrets Act.'

Gayhurst House, a sixteenth century manor house north of Milton Keynes, is now split into apartments, but it served as a Bletchley Park out-station from September 1942. (Colin Philpott)

Interestingly, Anne maintained her vow of secrecy, even when writing a book more than sixty years after the war ended and some time after the secrets of Bletchley Park were in the public domain. Her book is entitled *Off Duty!* and is a fascinating insight into life at Gayhurst but it does not contain any details of the actual work she did there.

Anne spoke of how the procedures and practices of naval life were maintained at Gayhurst even though it was about as far away from the sea as is possible in England. Wrens posted there wore naval uniform, naval language was used and naval marching drills took place. The living conditions were fairly spartan and the shift system was relentless, a rotating pattern of midnight to eight in the morning, eight until four and four to midnight. But she remembered with great affection the fun she and her fellow Wrens had in their spare time, particularly the thirty-six-hour breaks they enjoyed on the days between shift changes. They often used these breaks to get a pass out and make a quick trip to London. She also recalls the smuggling of alcohol for illicit parties at Gayhurst. After the war, Anne was a leading light in the world of ballooning and also published several books of poetry. She died in 2011.

Gayhurst, which is to the north of what is now Milton Keynes, is now converted into private apartments.

Stanmore. From 1942, an out-station was established at Stanmore in North-West London, which is believed to have housed forty-nine bombes, with accommodation for 400 staff.

Adstock. The out-station at Adstock Manor, to the west of Milton Keynes, was opened in March 1941 and housed five bombes.

Wavendon. The out-station at Wavendon House, on the east side of Milton Keynes, operated from March 1941 until January 1944. By then it had fourteen bombes but they were sent to other stations after its closure.

The original motivation for creating the out-stations seems to have been security. Spreading the codebreaking activity over several sites reduced the risk of disruption if one was taken out or disabled by enemy action. However, the concentration of so much of the activity later in the war at Eastcote and Stanmore was also part of a general move back to London which we will also observe in relation to other dispersed wartime facilities. As the threat of bombing in the capital reduced, the London-centric nature of the British establishment reasserted itself.

Some of the 200 staff, many of them members of the Women's Royal Naval Service known as Wrens, gathering outside Gayhurst House during the war. (Barbara Carter)

A final thought about Bletchley Park and its out-stations. Even with the testimony of veterans of 'the Park', it remains quite difficult for the twenty-first century mind to come to terms with the sense of duty which apparently protected the secrecy of the vital British codebreaking operation. How would so many intelligent, creative young people not ask too many questions and resist the temptation to talk about what they were doing? Much of the answer to that is simply that they were living in a very different age to our own.

'Y' Stations – Bletchley Park's Eyes and Ears

In order to do their work, Bletchley's codebreakers needed raw material and that raw material was the intercepts of enemy wireless communications. Across Britain and overseas and on ships at sea, there was a network of so-called 'Y' stations. The purpose of the interception was to access the content of messages, much of which was coded. Some of the 'Y' stations also had radio direction finding equipment to find the source of the messages. These 'Y' stations were run by a variety of different organisations including the Army, Royal Navy and the RAF.

There were 42 'Y' stations in Britain, including Scotland, Northern Ireland and Wales, but the majority were in England, mostly in the south and south-east. These included:

Beaumanor Hall, near Loughborough in Leicestershire. The present hall, built in the nineteenth century, was requisitioned by the War Office in 1939 and was put to various wartime uses including as one of the leading 'Y' stations. Throughout the war, the hall was the headquarters of the War Office 'Y' section. Although the interception activity was at first run from inside the main house, a twenty-acre field in the grounds was later identified for the construction of new huts to house the operation. The huts were all built with blast walls and all disguised to look like the outbuildings of an English stately home – as barns, cottages, a glasshouse and even a cricket pavilion. Intercepts gathered at Beaumanor were written out and transported at first by motorcycle courier to Bletchley Park and later by teleprinter using Post Office land lines. Most of the wireless listeners were women from the ATS (Auxiliary Territorial Service). Beaumanor was another example of a secret facility hidden in plain sight. Beaumanor Hall was bought by Leicestershire County Council in the 1970s and is now an events and conference centre. Many of the wartime buildings remain.

RAF Chicksands, Bedfordshire. Situated between Bedford and Luton near the twelfth-century monastery, Chicksands Priory, this was an important RAF-run intercept station. Joyce Davies, a WAAF who worked there during the war, told the BBC in 2005 that she found it very difficult to keep quiet about the work she did there. She worked there for three years and the station was involved in listening to enemy messages and in transmitting to agents behind enemy lines.

'We were more scared of the Official Secrets Act than of bombing', she said, 'But we were forbidden from discussing our work, even with our colleagues, and we obeyed.' A bomb did land in a nearby river, but harmlessly, and no one was hurt.

RAF Chicksands is still involved in intelligence work. It is now the headquarters of the Joint Intelligence Training Group. More than 5,000 armed services personnel and others, including police, receive intelligence training there.

Beaumanor Hall near Loughborough was the headquarters of the 'Y' station network of forty-two listening stations across the country which supplied material for Bletchley Park. Much of the operation took place in specially-constructed outbuildings in the grounds disguised to look like parts of a country estate. (Beaumanor Hall)

HMS Forest, near Harrogate, North Yorkshire was one of the more remote 'Y' stations situated on Blubberhouses Moor to the west of Harrogate. After the war, it became a Royal Navy high frequency receiver station. In 2003, the work was transferred to a private company which now provides a service to the Ministry of Defence from a nearby site. The original site has been converted into a school for children with behavioural, emotional and social needs, now known as Forest Moor School.

Scarborough, North Yorkshire. The original Scarborough site in Sandybed Lane had been a First World War wireless station for intercepting German naval messages. It became a 'Y' station at the start of the Second

World War charged with intercepting German naval messages and also with direction finding. In 1943 the station was moved to a bigger site on the location of the former Scarborough Racecourse where the new facilities were partly buried in a bunker. The site, rebuilt in the 1970s, is still in use today as an outpost of GCHQ.

Ivy Farm, Knockholt, near Sevenoaks in Kent. This 160-acre site was requisitioned on the North Downs not far from Sevenoaks and was operational by July 1942. Its purpose was to concentrate on trying to intercept German non-Morse radio traffic known as 'FISH'. British intelligence had become aware that the Germans were making increasing use of teleprinter traffic and needed a special station dedicated to trying to intercept these messages. Eventually, 815 people worked at the site which continued in operation until the 1950s.

As well as the network of 'Y' stations across the country, there were similar stations abroad including in India, Sri Lanka (then Ceylon), Egypt and Kenya as well as with mobile army units and on board ships. There were also a number of other important locations in Britain associated with the interception of enemy signals traffic and other related matters:

Arkley View, Barnet, London. Arkley View was a requisitioned country house in the village of Arkley near Barnet which had been established by the Post Office as a 'Y' station. However, it acquired a more celebrated role. With the cover address of 'Box 25, Barnet' it was taken over by the then Radio Security Service (RSS) as a base for the monitoring of illicit radio transmissions. The RSS had developed from an earlier organisation called the Illicit Wireless Intercept Organisation whose original purpose had been to monitor illegal radio transmissions inside Britain in peacetime. The RSS's first objective was to root out any radio messages from German agents who might be operating inside Britain. They also turned their attention to identifying radio transmissions from Germany and occupied Europe. An army of amateur radio enthusiasts were recruited as volunteer interceptors, known as VIs. They were mainly recruited from members of the Radio Society of Great Britain. Fifty volunteers were recruited early in the war and 600 German transmitters identified that led to the discovery and 'turning' of countless German agents.

Originally, the RSS had been based inside Wormwood Scrubs Prison in London as a security measure but, as the operation expanded and more space was needed, Arkley View was taken over. By 1941, over 10,000 message sheets a day were being sent by the VIs and interceptors employed directly

The requisitioned country house Arkley View with the code name of 'Box 25, Barnet' was a vital link in the Bletchley Park codebreaking operation, intercepting radio transmissions from German agents and later from German stations. Its equipment and records were destroyed at the end of the war and the house demolished. (Barnet Council)

by the RSS to Arkley. From there many were sent on to Bletchley Park for decoding. In effect Arkley became the centre of a massive civilian operation which worked alongside the military 'Y' station operation in providing intercepts of enemy communications. Arkley View's equipment and records were destroyed at the end of the war and the house demolished.

Hanslope Park, Milton Keynes, Buckinghamshire remains to this day a highly secret government centre. It is partly occupied by departments of the Foreign Office and by Her Majesty's Government Communication Centre. The latter is involved in research and development of communication systems and software for use in intelligence work. But Hanslope Park's origins as a secret location go back to 1941 when the seventeenth-century estate was requisitioned and became a base for a new radio intercept station for the RSS. It continued in that role throughout the rest of the war and remained an important government radio communications centre until the 1990s.

Windy Ridge, near Bletchley, Buckinghamshire. In a field near the church in the village of Whaddon, not far from Bletchley Park, there are virtually no visible remains of what was arguably the most important element in the chain of Britain's codebreaking operation. Two small huts contained a radio transmission centre and teleprinters for receiving information by landline from Bletchley Park. It was from here that messages were sent to commanders in the field providing them with the highly sensitive intelligence gleaned from the codebreaking operation. After the war the huts were given over to a local farmer but have since disappeared and only some concrete foundations remain.

Chain Home Radar

Worth Matravers, Isle of Purbeck, Dorset. Sitting in the Square and Compass Inn in the tiny Dorset village of Worth Matravers in the summer of 2017 was to be transported back three-quarters of a century. This 300-year-old pub was the watering hole for the wartime scientists who undertook pioneering research into the development of radar at the extensive clifftop complex developed on the nearby coastline. The pub contains some memorabilia from the time as a reminder of the brief period in the early 1940s when this quiet corner of Dorset was at the vanguard of developing technology that proved crucial to the outcome of the war.

From May 1940 to May 1942, Worth Matravers, on the Isle of Purbeck, was the effective headquarters of British radar research. Before the war, British researchers had created an early warning system known as the Chain Home Radar network. Today there is very little left to see at the site – a few foundations of buildings long since demolished and a memorial which acknowledges the important work that took place here. The memorial was unveiled by Sir Bernard Lovell in October 2001 and the Purbeck Radar Museum Trust, formed in 1991, preserves the memory

The Chain Home radar station on the Isle of Purbeck in Dorset was one of sixty sites around the country which formed part of the Dowding System of air defence. (Purbeck Radar Museum Trust)

of the site, and the wider story of wartime radar, through talks, exhibitions and other activities.

Worth Matravers was both a functioning radar station in its own right, one of a chain of over sixty sites around the coastline of Britain developed before and during the Second World War, but it was also a research site. There were a number of parts to the site. The radar station was set up on A-Site with two 75 metre wooden aerial towers. The scientists occupied B- and C-Sites which contained laboratories, another tower, as well as administrative offices, stores, workshops and the like. Later, other facilities were added including the building of the Chain Home Low radar. This was a response to the fact that tests just before the war started had shown that the existing Chain Home radar was not good at detecting low flying aircraft. This was a phenomenon that led to the phrase 'getting in under the radar' so higher frequency radar with aerials mounted on gantries just a few metres above ground were built to deal with this. At Worth Matravers a Chain Home Low aerial was first put up alongside the existing main aerials on A–Site but this did not produce good enough coverage. A new location, D–Site, was identified below the clifftop and this proved effective.

Among the most important developments of radar worked on at Worth Matravers was the cavity magnetron, a small but very powerful transmitter valve. Developed in 1940 at Birmingham University, this revolutionary advancement of radar technology was tested and further developed at Worth Matravers. It enabled radar to use shorter wavelengths to show target positions more accurately. This also meant smaller aerials were needed and this in turn meant that compact radar, particularly fitted in planes, could be employed as well as the huge aerials on the ground. This was just one of a number of important refinements and improvements made to Britain's radar systems during the two years that Britain's radar research was based on the Dorset coast.

However, the story of Second World War radar begins well before 1940 and well away from Dorset.

Daventry Experiment. Britain's first experience of bombardment from the air had occurred during the First World War. Britain had tracked enemy airships (Zeppelins) and aircraft by intercepting their wireless signals, but the only real attempt to use any sort of technology to give early warning of hostile aircraft was rather unsophisticated. Large sound locators, rather like giant eardrums, were built at various points on the English coast. In the mid-1930s when serious attention was being given to the threat of bombing in a future conflict, these sound locators were tested and found to be useless. Those who were arguing for air defences to be developed as a matter of urgency faced something of a battle. There was still a view in the military, and among many politicians, that defensive measures against aerial bombardment were rather futile. This was a view summarised in Stanley Baldwin's phrase 'the bomber will always get through'. Nevertheless, Air Chief Marshal Hugh Dowding, then in charge of air research, was persuaded to allow some research. In February 1935, an experiment was conducted near the BBC transmitters at Daventry which demonstrated that a bomber

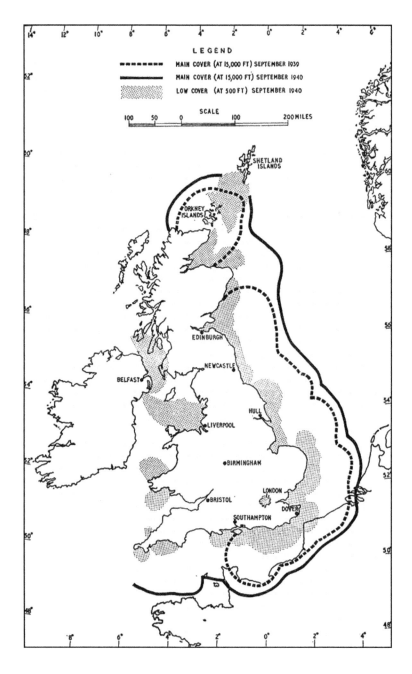

Map showing the extent of radar coverage of the coast of Britain in the early years of the war, distinguishing the main Chain Home radar capability and that of the Chain Home Low system designed to detect enemy aircraft at lower altitudes. (Purbeck Radar Museum Trust)

flying in the vicinity had reflected the radio signal from the transmitter and the idea of radar was practical.

Orfordness, Suffolk. Following the success of the Daventry experiment, money was provided to test the concept more fully over water. These tests took place at Orfordness on the Suffolk coast where earlier work on radio direction finding had taken place. During the summer of 1935, a number of tests showed that planes could be detected by radar up to a hundred miles away. These results accelerated the pace of development of radar with the building of an experimental chain of five stations and the establishment of a new centre for radar research and development. Meanwhile, Orfordness retained a military role throughout the Cold War with an Atomic Weapons Research Establishment established there. It is now a National Trust nature reserve.

Bawdsey Manor, Suffolk. The new centre for radar research which was established at Bawdsey Manor became known as RAF Bawdsey. From early 1936 until the beginning of the war, this was the headquarters of a rapidly expanding radar network. By the time of the Munich crisis in September 1938, the first five stations were fully operational and by 1939 the Chain Home Radar network provided coverage of the entire Europe-facing coastline of Britain from Scotland to the West Country.

Bawdsey itself was part of the Chain and it remained so throughout the war and beyond. RAF Bawdsey was eventually closed in 1991. It is now a PGL Holiday Centre but there is a museum commemorating its role in the history of radar which was reopened in 2018 after a refurbishment. Bawdsey can claim to be the birthplace of British radar, but its role as the centre for radar research came to an abrupt end when war broke out. It was deemed to be too vulnerable a location and the scientists were moved first to Dundee and then to Dorset and to Worth Matravers.

The Role of Radar. Eventually, there were over sixty Chain Home radar locations around Britain, some equipped with both the conventional high antennae and aerials and others also with the Chain Home Low equipment. They were a vital component of the Dowding System (described in Chapter Two), the integrated system of early warning information of enemy air attacks. The information came from radar, from visual observation (see the Royal Observer Corps below) and also later from airborne radar. It was linked to the RAF Fighter Command HQ at Bentley Priory and its lower level command centres via dedicated land lines. This provided a coherent way

RAF Bawdsey on the Suffolk coast was the centre of the Chain Home radar network from 1936 as the network developed. There is a now a museum on the site about the history of radar. (Imperial War Museum)

of maximising the chances of deploying fighter aircraft against incoming bombers in the most effective manner.

Doctor Phil Judkins of Leeds University is an expert in the history of radar and is in no doubt that radar played a crucial role in the outcome of the Battle of Britain, and also in subsequent phases of the war. Without the information provided by radar, Britain's aircraft and aircrews would have been exhausted and depleted more quickly. Standing patrols of fighter aircraft would have had to have been positioned speculatively to await incoming German bombers. With radar and the wider Dowding System, targeted use of planes was possible and, without this, the outcome of the Battle of Britain might have been different.

Secrecy of Radar. The issue of the security and secrecy of radar installations is a fascinating one. At face value, the appearance of a series of fairly conspicuous buildings and a number of very tall masts right on the coastline would seem difficult to conceal. Doctor Judkins believes that the key to understanding the security and secrecy of the various radar installations like Bawdsey and Worth Matravers is the differing British and German attitudes to the bombing threat and the value of radar.

Germany had also developed radar defences but these were not linked to the operational deployment of defensive fighter aircraft in the way that Britain did with the Dowding System. The mindset of the German High Command was very much offensive rather than defensive and greater emphasis was given to attack rather than defence. Even more crucially, the Germans failed to appreciate the full value of radar in the British defensive system.

They were aware of the development of radar by Britain from before the war. Although the work at Orfordness and at Bawdsey pre-1939 was deemed to be highly secret, there was plenty of information in the public domain about the work. The address and staff details of Bawdsey Research Station appeared in official publications. Pictures of Bawdsey's aerials were on holiday postcards sold in the area. Books about radio research written by the radar scientists were available in bookshops. Despite some scepticism from Hermann Göring as overall boss of the Luftwaffe, the Germans did send reconnaissance flights along the British coast, including using Zeppelin airships. However, they misinterpreted what they observed and concluded that the masts and aerials along the British coast were simply wireless direction-finding stations, like those used in the First World War.

Despite this conclusion, the Luftwaffe did bomb RAF Chain Home radar installations in the early stages of the Battle of Britain in the summer of 1940. The stations at **Dover, Rye, Pevensey** and at **Ventnor** on the Isle of Wight were attacked on 12 August. Ventnor was badly damaged and put out of action for a week. However, its wooden huts rather than its masts were damaged and reserve equipment was brought into operation using the undamaged aerials. Even before the war, most Chain Home stations had been provided with 'buried reserve' stations in case of attack.

Doctor Judkins believes that the secrecy of the research activity at Worth Matravers was maintained. In many ways, it was yet another example of something hidden in plain sight. From the air, the establishment might well have looked like yet another military camp with no particular clue that some of Britain's top scientists were working there on developing radar still further. Worth Matravers was a pretty remote site (as had been Orfordness and Bawdsey Manor) and like Bletchley Park and other secret establishments, the vast majority of the people working there would have kept quiet about what they were doing. He also thinks that local people would have just regarded it as 'something important to do with the war' and not asked many questions. There was also a direct economic benefit to the local community. The nearest town of Swanage and other nearby places, denuded of nearly all of their holiday trade because of the war, would have been very pleased to have had the scientists and others billeted with them.

Nevertheless, despite all this, in 1942, all of a sudden, it was decided to move the research components of Worth Matravers in great haste. British Commandos had raided a German radar station on the French coast at Bruneval. Then British intelligence had reported a build-up of German paratroops near Cherbourg on the French coast and it was feared they might be planning a raid on the radar base in Dorset. It was decided to move the scientists and their equipment to Malvern in Worcestershire and it was done very quickly. It is said that the Ministry of Defence requisitioned the entire Pickford's removal fleet and conducted the move in a weekend!

Worth Matravers remained a radar station throughout the rest of the war and beyond. The last tower was taken down in the mid-1970s. **Malvern** remained the centre of British radar development until the end of the war.

Other sites

As the bombing threat from the Luftwaffe reduced after 1942, some of the Chain Home Radar network was stood down. Also, even before the end of the war, newer, more sophisticated technologies were being developed. Chain Home, which employed huge fixed, rather than rotating aerials, was by then seen as a rather crude system and was largely deemed outdated by 1945. It was eventually replaced by a new system called ROTOR in the 1950s. However, the emerging demands of the Cold War did mean that some refurbished Chain Home stations were kept in service through the late 1940s and into the 1950s.

In 2018 there are very few physical remains of the Chain Home network whose lifespan was short-lived but which played a crucial role at a decisive moment in history. Among the locations worth mentioning are:

RAF Staxton Wold near Scarborough, North Yorkshire can arguably be described as the oldest surviving operational radar station in the world. It was operational from April 1939 as part of the Chain Home network and is still in use today as a remote radar head station.

The small village of Dunkirk in Kent is one of very few Second World War radar sites still recognisable. One of the anti-aircraft gun emplacements on the site has now been converted into a private dwelling. (Neocribs)

RAF Stenigot, Lincolnshire remained in use as a radar station until the 1980s and was largely demolished in the 1990s. Its tower is a listed building and has been used by the RAF as a training facility for aerial building.

Blackpool Tower, Lancashire was even used as a Chain Home Radar receiving station for a short time to monitor the Irish Sea from April 1941. A 12 metre section of the Tower was replaced by a wooden structure allowing for the housing of aerials.

Dunkirk near Faversham, Kent. This radar station, which is one of the few remaining Chain Home sites, was sold at auction in 2012, and is now owned by a private company which rents out the one remaining mast for phone and radio communication dishes. Many of the buildings from the Second World War remain and one of the gun emplacements has been converted into a private house.

Coldingham, Scottish Borders. Drone Hill at Coldingham in the Scottish Borders was the first Chain Home station in Scotland and it came into operation in early 1939. After the war it became RAF Crosslaw and also an important Cold War centre, the location of a government nuclear bunker. The site is now a caravan park but some of the Second World War buildings remain.

Royal Observer Corps

Finally, a brief mention of one often overlooked element of Britain's early warning defences – the Royal Observer Corps. This was a force of around 10,000, mainly civilian, volunteers who carried out visual observation of the skies to spot and recognise incoming aircraft. The Corps had its origins in 1925 when it was set up as the Observer Corps to report aircraft and coastal shipping movements and report them to the defence organisations. Initially, the observers were volunteers and they were recruited by the police with the status of special constables.

During the Second World War volunteers tended to be older people, too old to fight in the front line, or people in reserved occupations. People as young as fifteen were also recruited. The volunteer force included a significant proportion of women. During the war, the Corps was managed by some full-time officers and it came under the aegis of the Air Ministry. At first observation posts were often literally in garden sheds next to a telegraph pole enabling a phone link to be made to a control centre. Later more substantial brick-built posts were established in all manner of places – on cliff tops, on the top of hills, and on the roofs of factories and public buildings.

In 1941 the Corps was awarded a 'Royal' epithet in recognition of its contribution to the Dowding System of air defence during the Battle of Britain. Hugh Dowding himself said that the contribution of the ROC was critical, 'The ROC constituted the whole means of tracking enemy aircraft once they had crossed the coastline. Their role was invaluable.'

The Royal Observer Corps continued into the Cold War. It was envisaged that it would have played a role in the aftermath of a nuclear attack. There is a small museum in Winchester in Hampshire commemorating the history of the ROC.

Tell-tale signs of the former life of this caravan site on the moors above Coldingham in the Scottish Borders, once the location of the first Chain Home Radar station in Scotland. (Colin Philpott)

P.C. 'Lofty' Austin, a former professional footballer with Tottenham Hotspur, and E.C. 'Smudge' Smith at a Royal Observer Corps post at Kings Langley in Hertfordshire. (Imperial War Museum)

Chapter Four

Broadcasting and Propaganda

The BBC's Dispersal – Wood Norton, Bristol, Bangor, Bedford,
'The Stronghold', 200 Oxford Street, 'Emergency News House',
Guerrilla Radio Stations, Transmitters; Black Propaganda Stations,
Other Communication Bases.

BBC Dispersal

The BBC was still a very young organisation, not yet twenty years old, when war broke out in 1939. The conflict immediately threw up some existential challenges for the Corporation. The most crucial was its relationship with the government and the military. Had it been down to the Air Ministry, the BBC might have been closed down altogether. Some people in the Ministry believed that radio transmitters would be an aid to navigation for German bombers and therefore broadcasting should cease. In addition, some politicians, particularly Winston Churchill after he became Prime Minister in 1940, saw the war as a time to get even with the BBC which he distrusted. As the war developed, the BBC had to work out its precise role. Was it part of the wartime propaganda and morale-boosting machinery of government? Was it to be an impartial news provider? How should it relate to the overtly propagandist broadcasting stations aimed at the Axis powers which the British Government set up? So, the BBC faced big battles, both technological and political, and the way the organisation navigated its way through these minefields would determine not only whether it had a 'good war' but also its longer-term future.

The BBC also faced a series of practical challenges in order to protect itself against the perceived threats of bombing and even sabotage. Work on addressing these issues had begun in the mid-1930s. As early as 1935, the BBC surveyed all its premises around the country and spent £50,000 (around £3million at 2018 prices) improving security and protection. Measures undertaken included more security fencing and installing steel shutters.

From 1938, however, as the likelihood of war increased, the BBC decided it would need to follow the principle of dispersal also undertaken by many other sectors of British life in wartime. This would both enable it to carry on broadcasting if its main headquarters at Broadcasting House in London were put out of action, but also provide for the safety of its staff. The evacuation and dispersal policy led to the creation of new studio and production facilities outside London, but also in the capital.

Wood Norton Hall, near Evesham, Worcestershire. Once owned by the last pretender to the throne of France, the Duke of Orléans, this Victorian stately home, set in the rolling hills of Worcestershire, was bought by the BBC in the spring of 1939. It was chosen because it was fairly remote, had extensive tree cover, and had enough space in the grounds for the discreet construction of temporary buildings. The purchase and conversion of Wood Norton was apparently done in secret. Rumours that the house was being prepared as a home for the Duke of Windsor, who as Edward VIII had abdicated three years earlier, and his wife were apparently encouraged by the BBC. However, a BBC engineer visiting a radio exhibition in Berlin in 1939 discovered that the Germans were aware of the BBC's purchase of the hall.

During late August and early September of 1939, frantic work was carried out to prepare the facilities at Wood Norton. The first BBC staff moved there on 29 August and the new control room was operational on Tuesday 5 September, two days after Britain declared war on Germany. The Music Production, Schools, Features and Drama departments all moved there in the early days of the war. By early 1940, Wood Norton had become one of the biggest broadcasting centres in Europe, producing 1,300 programme items per week amounting to 835 hours of radio.

The number of people working for the BBC increased dramatically during the war from fewer than 5,000 in 1939 to over 11,000 by 1942. At the height of its operation in 1941, about 28 per cent of the BBC's workforce was based at Wood Norton. The BBC Monitoring Service, which was set up in 1939 to monitor foreign radio broadcasts, was also based at Wood Norton until 1943. The BBC took over other neighbouring properties and staff were billeted in the nearby town of Evesham. Wood Norton was never bombed although a fire, apparently started accidentally in September 1940, caused some damage although little interruption to programme making.

In 1941 emergency studios were built on the lawn at Wood Norton in case the intensity of bombing in London necessitated moving live broadcasting out of the capital. However, that did not happen and Wood Norton's wartime

Staff of the BBC's Monitoring Service working at Wood Norton Hall during the early part of the Second World War. The Hall, near Evesham, was the BBC's main base outside London during the conflict. (BBC)

Wood Norton Hall is now a hotel although the BBC still retains training facilities and emergency underground broadcasting facilities in the grounds. (Wood Norton Hall Hotel)

role remained as a dispersed production facility and as a potential evacuation centre for Broadcasting House. From late 1941 onwards, activity at the Worcestershire site began to wane. The Monitoring Department moved to Caversham in Berkshire in 1943. Other departments also left Wood Norton, partly because it was not popular with some staff. Music and Schools went to Bristol and Features and Drama to Manchester.

However, after the war, Wood Norton lived on as an important BBC base. It became the BBC's Engineering Training Centre and generations of BBC engineers and others, including the author, passed through its portals on BBC courses of one sort or another. In the 1960s, it acquired a Cold War role when an underground emergency studio complex was constructed at the site. Known as 'PAWN' (Protected Area Wood Norton), its existence has never been officially confirmed or denied by the BBC but it was designed for use in the event of nuclear war. Even though the BBC sold off Wood Norton Hall, which is now a hotel, it retains its training facilities and emergency studio in the grounds there.

BBC Bristol. The West Country city was another important wartime base for the BBC. The BBC Symphony Orchestra and the BBC Theatre Orchestra moved to Bristol at the beginning of the war. They stayed there for a year using local facilities, including Colston Hall. Light Music, Entertainment, Listener Research and various administrative departments also went to Bristol. Almost 13 per cent of BBC staff were there in 1941 and the BBC used a variety of premises, including church halls, as bases for studios and offices. However, Bristol was subject to heavy bombing and further dispersal became necessary. Light Entertainment moved temporarily to the Winter Gardens in Weston-Super-Mare, but later to Bangor. The Symphony Orchestra moved to Bedford in 1941.

However, the most remarkable aspect of the BBC's wartime activity in Bristol was the building of an emergency studio centre in the Clifton Rocks Railway Tunnel. The BBC took over the disused tunnels of a former funicular railway which had linked the river level of the Avon gorge with the district of Clifton some 120 metres higher. Studios and control rooms were constructed on seven levels and they were staffed continuously from 1942 until the end of the war as an emergency alternative to Broadcasting House, London for live broadcasting. They were never needed for this purpose, but the studios were used for recording and routing programmes.

BBC Bangor. One of the impacts of the war on the BBC was the need for it to provide popular entertainment to take people's minds off the awfulness of the conflict. This meant that the BBC's rather highbrow cultural tastes pre-war had to be modified. One of the best-loved of these programmes was

The derelict remains of studios created in the disused tunnels of the Clifton Ricks Railway in Bristol – yet another of the BBC's emergency resources outside London. (Nick Catford)

'ITMA' or 'It's that Man Again'. Starring Tommy Handley, it was a comedy show that poked fun at the Nazis and also at British officialdom. It ran for 300 episodes through the war and continued until 1949. It was tremendously popular and even the King was said to be a regular listener. It spawned many famous catchphrases which persist to this day like 'I don't mind if I do' and 'Can I do you now, Sir?' and much-loved comedy characters like Mrs Mopp and Colonel Chinstrap.

In fact, unknown to the audience at the time, the show was recorded not in London but in Bangor in North Wales. The BBC's Light Entertainment Department decamped there from Bristol in 1940 and stayed until 1943. Around 400 BBC staff were based in Bangor and many wartime stars like

Bangor was the wartime home of the BBC's Light Entertainment Department from 1940 to 1943 and 400 staff worked there at Bryn Meirion studios which were opposite the current BBC Bangor base. (Unknown)

Vera Lynn and Arthur Askey passed through. In 1943, when the threat of bombing in London had receded, the operation was moved back to the capital. It was said that it was difficult to get some stars to travel to Bangor. The current BBC Bangor studios are opposite the site where the BBC's wartime programmes were made.

BBC Bedford. The final main out-of-London centre which was important in the BBC's wartime story was Bedford. In 1941, the Music Department, including the BBC's orchestras went there. Heavy bombing necessitated a move away from Bristol and the BBC investigated several possible new bases, eventually choosing Bedford. A special train took orchestra members from Bristol to Bedford in August 1941. Later several other BBC departments including Religion were also relocated to Bedford.

A number of premises around the town were used by the BBC including the Bunyon Hall schoolrooms, the Castle Billiard Hall, the Corn Exchange, Bedford School Hall and St Paul's Church from where the Daily Service was broadcast. Some of the BBC Prom concerts took place in Bedford.

Other BBC sites outside London. Manchester hosted the Features and Drama departments after they left Wood Norton. A temporary studio was created in a theatre below the main library. Other BBC departments went to Glasgow and Oxford. Many of the BBC's pre-existing regional studios continued to play a role in the Corporation's programming. Even though they had no dedicated local programmes during the war, they contributed programmes to the national service.

BBC Broadcasting House, London and its 'Stronghold'. The art-deco edifice which remains the headquarters of the BBC as it approaches its centenary had been opened in 1932. During the war, Broadcasting House was affected directly by bombing on two occasions. The most serious was on 15 October 1940 when seven people were killed and there was extensive internal damage. However, the overall structure of the building remained secure. Broadcasting operations were barely disrupted and Bruce Belfrage famously carried on reading the nine o'clock news bulletin after a brief pause as though nothing had happened. On 8 December of the same year a land mine exploded outside Broadcasting House, killing a policeman and causing some damage to a studio and other facilities.

Despite these incidents, Broadcasting House remained operational throughout the war. The emergency evacuation facilities put in place in Wood Norton and in Bristol were never needed. However, the BBC took no chances and, as well as the out-of-London emergency studios, built another underneath Broadcasting House. After the experience of the 1940–1941 Blitz in London (and the bombing of Broadcasting House itself), the BBC decided that it needed a secure refuge for its news and current affairs operation in the capital.

Work was completed in November 1942 on a single storey structure with base, walls and roof almost 2 metres thick and designed to withstand 500lb bombs. It was built on the site of a proposed extension to Broadcasting House which had been planned pre-war but postponed. The Stronghold, as the new complex was known, contained four news studios with associated control rooms and its own generator and other supplies. It was also sealed against a gas attack. The Stronghold was never needed and it was subsequently incorporated into post-war extensions of Broadcasting House.

Other BBC London Premises. The BBC made use of a number of other London premises during the war. These included:

The BBC's headquarters of Broadcasting House in central London survived the war and has subsequently been redeveloped several times. It was hit twice by bombing in October and December 1940, but it remained in use throughout the war so that many of the BBC's emergency locations were never needed. (Stephen Craven)

The Aeolian Halls in Bond Street. These were used for concerts and recitals after the destruction by an incendiary bomb on 10 May 1941 of the Queen's Hall. This was right next to Broadcasting House and had been London's principal concert venue and also home of the BBC Proms.

The Paris Cinema, the Monseigneur Cinema and the Criterion Theatre were also used. All were at least partially underground and therefore considered safer.

200 Oxford Street was part of the Peter Robinson department store and was a base for the BBC's External Services. Requisitioned by the BBC in 1941, it became operational in June 1942 with studios and control rooms 15 metres below ground.

Emergency News House and Guerrilla Radio Stations. The lengths to which the BBC went in secret to provide for every wartime eventuality can be illustrated by one last set of premises worth mentioning. As well as Wood Norton, the Bristol tunnels and the London Stronghold, former BBC engineers have spoken about the existence of yet more standby facilities for maintaining news broadcasts in the event of major bomb damage in central London. A large Victorian house in **Woodside Avenue, Finchley in North-West London** was kitted out as the Emergency News House. In the BBC, this went by the name of Kelvedon and had a control room in the basement, two small news studios, its own generator and lines linking it into the BBC's transmission system. It was apparently kept on standby and visited by BBC engineers regularly to check that everything was working. The BBC occupied the house from May 1940 until June 1946, although it was sub-let to the Canadian Forces Network towards the end of the war. Ironically, the house was itself damaged in an air raid in January 1941.

As well as this London facility, there were a series of premises identified and equipped around the country which could be turned into 'guerrilla' radio stations in the event of widespread devastation across the country or enemy invasion. A series of facilities were equipped in **London (in Marylebone Road and Portland Place), in Kidderminster, Ponteland near Newcastle, Penketh near Warrington, Aberdare in Wales and in Edinburgh and Glasgow** from which such stations would have been operated.

Transmitters

In order to allay Air Ministry fears about the possible use of transmitters as navigational aids for enemy bombers, the BBC came up with a scheme which placated the military and maintained broadcasting. The transmitters could be, and were, taken off air. Part of the agreement between the Ministry and the BBC allowed RAF Fighter Command to shut down particular transmitters during air raids. Dedicated phone lines were put in between BBC control rooms and Fighter Command headquarters to allow this to happen.

However, to maintain continuity of service, the BBC proposed concentrating all domestic radio broadcasts via just two groups of transmitters all using the same frequency. This meant that, if a particular transmitter had to be taken off air, listeners would still be able to get the service from another neighbouring transmitter. It was this, incidentally, which meant, though, that separate pre-war regional services had to be abandoned and subsumed into the national service which became known as the Home Service, later to become Radio Four.

As a further means of alleviating the impact of this arrangement, a network of supposedly secret low-power medium wave transmitters was also gradually developed across the country with a range of only about ten miles. These 'Group H' network transmitters were generally set up on public buildings, often using water towers or other structures as masts. Their control rooms were generally underground. They were able to broadcast the BBC Home Service in specific localities when a main transmitter was off air. They were also developed with the idea that they might be localised radio stations in the event of catastrophic bombing damage or invasion. Some of the 'Group H' transmitter sites were retained for post-war use.

Black Propaganda Stations

We have chronicled the lengths to which the BBC went to maintain its ability to broadcast during wartime and seen how some of its precautions were not in fact needed. Those who have studied the BBC's role during the Second World War and its relationship with Government in particular, have generally concluded that it ended up steering a good course. There were lots of arguments along the way and many classic British fudges and compromises. Asa Briggs, in his *History of Broadcasting in the United Kingdom* concluded that the BBC 'retained throughout the war a very substantial measure of independence'. Edward Stourton, in *Auntie's War* asserts that the BBC 'was allowed to go on telling...the exact truth, every detail of it because it worked, and it helped Britain win.'

However, the BBC was not independent and impartial in the way we might understand these concepts in the twenty-first century. It was, like the rest of the media, subject to censorship and it withheld details in its news reporting that were deemed helpful to the enemy, for example, the precise location of bombing raids. It was very straightforwardly involved in

Bundesarchiv, B 145 Bild-F005102-0003
Foto: Steiner, Egon | Februar 1958

Selmer Defton, the German-born British journalist, who became the leading light in the conception and operation of 'black propaganda' radio stations broadcast from Britain aimed at Germany and other countries. (Bundesarchiv)

morale-boosting and public information broadcasting in conjunction with the Ministry of Information. This included broadcasts linked to Ministry of Information campaigns about 'Digging for Victory' and advice on how to make best use of rationed foods.

However, in its reporting, it came to realise, and politicians came to accept, that generally, telling people the truth was the best way to maintain public confidence in the conduct of the war. There is some evidence that, at the beginning of the war, the public expected the BBC to be a government mouthpiece. However, the broadcasting of what was regarded as reliable news and also the rather self-deprecating approach of entertainment shows like 'ITMA' somehow made people feel that the BBC was on their side.

All of the above applied to the domestic broadcasting of the BBC and, for the most part, to the news programmes broadcast by the BBC's External Services which expanded enormously during the war. However, the BBC did have to live cheek by jowl with the darker arts of broadcasting and communication which Britain engaged in, aimed at Germany and other enemy countries. BBC external stations were involved in broadcasting coded messages to the French Resistance and other groups. The boundaries between 'black' and 'white' broadcasting were sometimes blurred.

Under the aegis of the Political Warfare Executive (PWE), established in 1941 to co-ordinate propaganda aimed at the Axis powers, Britain engaged in a variety of propaganda exercises, most of them based from locations in that 'spooks triangle' around what is now Milton Keynes. As an aside, it is remarkable how large a concentration of the locations featured in this book, especially those of a particularly clandestine nature, were in that area. There are three likely explanations. This was the favoured north side of London, perceived to be less vulnerable to air attacks than the other side of London. There was a plentiful supply of suitable country houses and estates which could be requisitioned. And perhaps also, like attracts like – there was some sense in these types of resources, and the people working in them, being close to each other.

These were the main Black Propaganda locations:

Woburn Abbey, Bedfordshire was the headquarters of the Political Warfare Executive. Its cover name was the Political Intelligence Department. Like many clandestine operations, the PWE HQ had a fake mailing address based in London. It was staffed from the Ministry of Information, the Special

Operations Executive and the BBC. From the riding school and stable block at Woburn, the PWE co-ordinated a range of propaganda materials aimed at Germany and also at German-occupied countries. The two main means of propaganda were leaflets and radio broadcasts.

Bush House, London. Bush House was built in stages from the 1920s and completed in 1935 as a multi-purpose office block and trade centre. A studio had been built there in a basement in the mid-1930s and was used by stations like Radio Luxembourg. In 1941 the BBC acquired this studio and later considerable other accommodation in the building, and based its European Services there. Later, some of the PWE staff and leadership transferred to Bush House in London and worked alongside the BBC there. Edward Stourton memorably talks about Bush House as the place where 'one lift…led to a world where truth was king, another to a world dedicated to deception and treachery'. After the war, Bush House became the headquarters of the BBC World Service and continued there until 2012. The building is now used by King's College, London.

Milton Bryan, Bedfordshire. It was from this small Bedfordshire village close to the Woburn Estate that some of the black propaganda radio stations broadcast. The purpose-built studio complex came on stream in 1943 with the ability to broadcast live. One station, '*Soldatensender Calais*', pretended to be a real German station particularly aimed at German soldiers. It mixed genuine news about Germany with false information, all designed to weaken the morale of the soldiers and to try to encourage them to surrender. It broadcast music of which the Nazi regime would disapprove. Sometimes it used the same frequencies as genuine German stations after they had gone off air. Another station, '*Deutscher Kurzwellensender Atlantik*', was aimed at the German Navy.

These stations, and others, were masterminded by Selmer Defton, a German-born British national who had worked as the *Daily Express* correspondent in Berlin before the war. In fact, at that time, both Britain and Germany thought he was a spy for the other side. However, he returned to Britain and became the leading light in the dark arts of black radio propaganda. The radio station was run by a mixture of British people, German prisoners of war and defectors, but all pretended to be German. They lived together in a large Victorian house called The Rookery in the Bedfordshire village of Aspley Guise.

Remains of the studios at Milton Bryan in Bedfordshire which came into operation in 1943 to transmit 'black propaganda' stations like 'Soldatensender Calais' aimed at fermenting discord among German soldiers. (Jayembee1969)

Much of the structure of the radio studio complex remains and the building is now used by a local scout group.

Wavendon Tower, Milton Keynes, Buckinghamshire. Wavendon Tower is a country house in the village of Wavendon, now part of Milton Keynes. It was the first black propaganda station base. Programmes were recorded here and then taken on discs to be transmitted from nearby transmitters.

One of the stations which was initially recorded at Wavendon was '*Gustav Siegfried Eins*' which broadcast from May 1941 until October 1943. The station's ruse was that it was the voice of a clandestine German military organisation and its leader, '*Der Chef*' played by a German émigré called Peter Seckelmann, who had fled Berlin in 1938. The idea

Now the offices of several companies, Wavendon Tower was the first base for
black propaganda radio stations organised by the Political Warfare Executive.
In the 1960s and 1970s the building was used as the headquarters of the Milton
Keynes Development Corporation. (Colin Philpott)

was that this radio station was a communication between the leader and
members of his group. Its tone was a clever mixture of loyalty to the
German military and the fatherland but undermining the reputation of
Nazi officials.

Wavendon became redundant when the more sophisticated facilities of
Milton Bryan became available. After the war, it had various uses, including
being the home of the Milton Keynes Development Corporation in the
1960s and 1970s. It is now used as offices.

Aspidistra, Crowborough, East Sussex. The coming on stream of
Milton Bryan studio coincided with the development of a massive new
radio transmitter ordered secretly, and initially without the knowledge of
the BBC, in the Ashdown Forest near Crowborough in East Sussex. The

650KW medium wave transmitter was bought from the United States in May 1941 at a cost of over £11,000 (over £5million at 2018 prices). Its code name of 'Aspidistra' was taken from the Gracie Fields' song about 'the biggest aspidistra in the world'. It was at the time the most powerful radio transmitter in the world.

The idea was to give the Political Warfare Executive a powerful new tool for aiming its black propaganda at enemy countries. Construction took place in 1942 and the new facility was operational by November of that year. The BBC was initially furious about the development of Aspidistra and argued that it should control the new facility which would enable it to provide more powerful transmissions of its services aimed at Europe. The BBC had been building its own new high-power transmitter at Ottringham in East Yorkshire which was beset with construction problems and came on stream late in 1943. Aspidistra was used principally for black propaganda, although some BBC broadcasts were also transmitted from there.

After the war, Aspidistra became a BBC facility for use by the World Service. It continued until 1984. Since then the transmitter has been dismantled and the buildings are now used by Sussex Police for training purposes.

Other Important Communication Bases

There are a number of important locations associated, not with broadcasting, but with other aspects of communication in Second World War Britain which deserve brief mentions.

SIGSALY, Oxford Street, London. The unlikely setting of a basement 60 metres below Selfridge's Department Store in Oxford Street, central London was the location of one of the most important communication links of the Second World War. It was here that the top secret SIGSALY trans-Atlantic communications link from Britain to the United States was based.

The technology, developed in the US, was a precursor of the digital communications technology that now enables mobile phone communication across the world. It was huge, requiring forty racks of equipment, needing 30,000 Watts of power and using around 230 square metres of floor space. It was simply too big to be installed in the Cabinet War Rooms. Instead, the Selfridge's basement was used because the Americans had already established

Logo of the Aspidistra transmitter, which became operational in 1942 providing a 650KW medium wave transmitter for the Political Warfare Executive's 'black propaganda' radio stations but later also used by the BBC. (Unknown)

a communications centre there. There was an underground cable link from there to Churchill's War Room.

Prior to the development of SIGSALY, Churchill and Roosevelt used analogue scrambler telephones for their conversations, but these were not secure and post-war evidence suggests the Germans were able to intercept many such conversations between the British Prime Minister and the US President. With SIGSALY, anyone trying to eavesdrop on the conversations heard only a buzzing noise. Fewer than twenty-five of the most senior British political and military leaders were security-cleared to use the link. It was this system that Churchill and Roosevelt used for most of their trans-Atlantic conversations from 1943 onwards. Eventually, more than a dozen SIGSALY terminals were established around the world and used for high-level military communications. After the war the equipment was removed from Selfridge's and returned to the United States. The system remained a secret until the 1970s.

Porthcurno. The small Cornish village of Porthcurno played a key role in Britain's communications infrastructure during the war. In 1870 Porthcurno

After the war, the Aspidistra site at Crowborough in East Sussex was used by the BBC World Service until 1984. The site is now used as a training facility by Sussex Police. (Nick Catford)

had become the nerve centre for a network of submarine telegraph cables linking Britain with a variety of other countries. At the beginning of the Second World War, the strategic importance of these links was recognised as being crucial to the war effort. As a result, their security was strengthened by the boring of two tunnels into the neighbouring cliffside to turn what had been an overground facility into an underground one.

It took a year of night and day work to complete the conversion during 1940 and 1941. The tunnel doors were bomb-proof and gas-proof and elaborate camouflaging took place to make the visible parts of the structure look like a belt of trees. The whole area was designated a high security one and local people were apparently largely unaware of just how much of the telegraph communication between Britain and its Allies passed through the place. It is said that more than 8million words passed through Porthcurno during the war. The Porthcurno Telegraph Station closed in 1993 and is now a museum.

A display at the National Cryptologic Museum in Maryland about the highly secure transatlantic phone system developed during the war and used by Churchill and Roosevelt for many of the conversations after 1943. (National Cryptologic Museum)

'Q' Central – RAF Leighton Buzzard, Bedfordshire was described in 1942 as the largest telephone exchange in the world. Known as 'Q' Central, it provided the communications infrastructure for much of the clandestine work centred on Bedfordshire, Buckinghamshire and the surrounding counties. Opened in 1939, with 600 staff, it handled the country's teleprinter network, much of the voice telephone network, as well as the RAF's communications. This included the routing of the communications related to the Chain Home Radar network. It was chosen because of its central location, the fact that it was well inland and not close to anything of obvious military significance. After the war, it continued under the name RAF Stanbridge as a major RAF communications base. Later it became a logistics centre for the RAF, but it closed in 2012 and has since been redeveloped for housing.

An estimated 8million words passed through the telegraph station at Porthcurno in Cornwall during the war, a key component of the Allies' worldwide communication system. Porthcurno is now a museum about telegraphy. (Unknown)

Rugby Radio Station, Rugby, Warwickshire. The twelve 250-metre-high radio masts dominating the Warwickshire skyline were an unmissable landmark for travellers on the M1 motorway for many years. They began life as a telegraph station in 1926 and later became a radio transmitting station. The first trans-Atlantic call to the United States went via Rugby in 1927. It was an important base for military communications during the Second World War. In January 1940 one of the masts there collapsed under the weight of ice and in March 1943 a serious fire put the transmitter out of action. These threats to the security of the Rugby station led to the search for a back-up facility. Rugby maintained a military role after the war but is now no more. Its masts were demolished in 2007 and the area has been redeveloped mainly for housing and a business park.

Criggion Radio Transmitting Station, near Welshpool, Powys, Wales was developed as a back-up facility for Rugby and first used in 1942. It took over completely from Rugby after the fire there in 1943 and for a six-month period it was the main facility for Britain's communication with its naval fleet. After the war it maintained a role in naval communications and is widely believed to have been used for communication with Britain's Trident nuclear submarines. Criggion closed in the 1990s and its masts were demolished in 2003. There have been plans to turn it into a museum but, as of 2018, these had not been realised.

Criggion Radio Station near Welshpool became the main communications base for Britain's naval fleet after a major fire at the Rugby station put that facility out of action. (Jonathan Davies)

Overall Assessment

It is quite difficult to assess the exact impact of propaganda radio stations aimed at enemy countries. However, it is perhaps telling that the Nazis' propaganda chief, Joseph Goebbels, admitted on several occasions how effective he thought it had been. The role of the BBC, both as a domestic and as an overseas broadcaster, was clearly of great importance.

What is also noteworthy is the secrecy around the broadcasting operations. Although, of course, the programmes emanating from all these radio stations were quite deliberately not secret, the bases from which they were broadcast remained secure throughout the war. Even the BBC's Broadcasting House in London, obviously a well-known and very visible broadcasting centre, remained in operation and indeed became one of the iconic symbols of British resilience.

Chapter Five

Decoys, Dummies and D-Day

Decoy Sites Night-time and Daytime; 'Starfish' sites protecting cities;
Dummy Factories and Towns; D-Day Deceptions; D-Day Rehearsals

Lullingstone Decoys, Lullingstone, Kent

In early 1940, Eric Lever was called up and underwent training to become part of an RAF ground crew. During the training in Blackpool, he was told that he was to be posted to one of the RAF's best-known stations, Biggin Hill in Kent.

'When I knew that I was being posted to Biggin Hill, I thought how lucky I was to be sent to a Fighter Command airfield. But three weeks later, I was told I wasn't actually being sent to Biggin Hill but to a place called Lullingstone – somewhere I had never heard of!' recalled Eric to *Kent Life* back in 2010 not long before he died. He was then sent on an electrical wiring course before finally arriving in Lullingstone with twelve other airmen. Eric and his colleagues were to be involved, not as ground crew looking after fighter planes at Biggin Hill, but in a way they had not expected – defending the airfield.

Eric's story, and that of the Lullingstone decoy, is a small part of one aspect of the secrecy of wartime Britain. Indeed, this aspect concerns something that was deliberately not secret, something that was intended to be highly visible in order to protect the secrecy of somewhere or something else. The operation to create such a deception was itself, of course, clouded in secrecy.

Lullingstone, near Sevenoaks in Kent was, and still is, famous for its castle which has been in the possession of the Hart-Dyke family for twenty generations. It sits in the Darenth Valley, an attractive area of countryside in the middle of the commuter belt which straddles south-east London and north-west Kent. In the 1930s, Lullingstone was proposed as one of four sites for the development of a new London airport and a railway station was built in anticipation of the arrival of the airport. The war put paid to the plan, London's subsequent post-war airport expansion happened elsewhere and the railway station was dismantled.

'Starfish' sites were developed to protect towns and cities by creating a visual impersonation of the place being protected so as to confuse Luftwaffe bombers. Eventually 237 Starfish sites protected eighty-one towns and cities around Britain. (St Margaret's, Richmond)

Nevertheless, the Darenth Valley ended up making a crucial contribution to Britain's military aviation capacity during the war and it hosted an airfield, albeit not a real one. It was only a few miles from Biggin Hill and was equipped and operational as a decoy site for Biggin Hill by March 1940. Its plain level valley bottom was ideal for creating a dummy airfield.

Eric Lever takes up the story:

> 'I was billeted to live at New Barn Cottage – a farm near Lullingstone Villa. Living on a farm, the food was good and plentiful as we were not really affected by rationing. Best of all I got friendly with the farmer's daughter and eventually, after the war, we got married. The farmer used his tractor to flatten out the humps and hillocks in the fields in the valley to make it look even more like an airfield.'

The first thing created in the fields at Lullingstone was a dummy airfield complete with runways, mock buildings and mock aircraft. Six mock Hurricane aircraft were constructed on site there. The aircraft were moved around to help add to the realism if German reconnaissance aircraft flew over the site. The real buildings needed to operate the decoy site, including huts for the operators, generator and telephone links, were hidden in a coppice. The idea was to create something close enough to the location of Biggin Hill to make German bombers think this was the real thing but far enough distant to draw the bombing away to somewhere relatively harmless.

Lullingstone's decoy was known as a 'K' station – a daytime decoy site. However, it also very soon after became what was known as a 'Q' station designed to provide a night time decoy as well. This was achieved by creating a series of lighting effects designed to make an area look like a runway. Yellow lights simulated a wind indicator, red lights were made to look like obstructions, white lights to simulate a runway and car headlamps to look like taxi-ing aircraft. All these lighting effects were controlled from a nearby bunker but the ground crew, like Eric Lever, took their orders by telephone landline from Biggin Hill itself.

At the height of the Battle of Britain, Biggin Hill was an important Luftwaffe target. The Lullingstone decoy site came into operation and a number of bombs landed quite close to it on 10, 15 and 22 September 1940. However, these were not necessarily an indication of the success of the decoy site. They were thought to be German bombers jettisoning their bombs on their way back home after raids on London.

Lullingstone acquired a third role as a decoy becoming one of the so-called Starfish sites. In spring of 1941, an adjacent site was equipped with oil tanks linked by troughs to stacks of wood and coal. The idea was to simulate fire and smoke to try to fool German bombers into thinking that their intended targets had already been hit. These Starfish sites were designed not to protect airfields but to protect towns and cities and some vital industrial installations. Lullingstone, although created as a decoy for Biggin Hill, was also on the flightpath of German bombers heading for London. It became one of a number of Starfish sites protecting the capital. When the order was given, the paraffin or diesel in the tanks was released onto burning coal creating a major fire and covering the area in black smoke.

Lullingstone's Starfish capability was used on a number of occasions. Eric Lever remembers one in particular, the night of 13 February 1944:

Lullingstone Castle in north-west Kent became an important decoy site protecting RAF Biggin Hill but also acting as a 'Starfish' decoy site to protect London. (Kent Life)

'I was on duty that night. It was a lovely clear night and we somehow knew it was going to be a night for enemy attacks. We got a call at about 8.30pm to light the dummy flarepath. About twenty minutes later, we could hear the drone of approaching aircraft, about twenty or thirty of them. They dropped flares which lit up the entire valley. Minutes later we heard the whistle of bombs and what turned out to be high explosive bombs had been dropped to the north-east of the site. The noise of the bombs was deafening even though they landed some way from the decoy site. A bit later there were further explosions. This was a baptism of fire for us as it was our first major experience of direct bombing. Trees and bushes burst into flame around where we were sheltering in our command bunker. We were then ordered to extinguish the flare path lights and just leave on the smaller lights which were supposed to resemble a bad blackout. A few more aircraft flew over but no further bombs were dropped, but it had been quite a night.'

The Kent countryside at Lullingstone where the wartime decoys and dummies were located, is now occupied by a golf course and a country park. (Glyn Baker)

The Lullingstone decoy site was dismantled at the end of the war. Today, the site of the Starfish decoy is a country park and the 'Q' decoy site is where Lullingstone Golf Course now stands. A few concrete hardstandings – the remains of the bunker, stores and other buildings – can be seen in and around some of the woodland.

Origins and Development of Decoys

The Lullingstone decoy story is a microcosm of a much bigger story. It was part of what became an elaborate network of deception across Britain during the war designed to defend airfields, factories, other key installations and eventually whole towns and cities from Luftwaffe bombers. Its origins lay in the pre-war debate about how to deal with the threat of bombing. The belief that 'the bomber will always get through', referred to earlier, shaped the approach to air defences during the 1930s. The prevailing RAF view was that the answer to the threat of German bombing was, in essence, that attack was the best form of defence. This meant a concentration on building up the RAF's fighting strength rather than too much emphasis on defensive measures against aerial bombardment.

It was only really in 1938 that serious attention was paid to the role of decoys as a means of defending Britain against air attacks. The first objective was to defend the growing number of airfields being built to accommodate the fighter and bomber aircraft whose numbers started to rise with the development of the Shadow Factory Scheme (see Chapter One). By the outbreak of war, there were a hundred airfields and the traditional protective measures were fairly rudimentary and simple. Buildings were camouflaged and, where possible, masked by tree cover. There was as much separation as possible between buildings so as to reduce the risk of fire spreading if one building was hit. Aircraft tended to be dispersed across the airfields rather than stored in hangars and aircraft were sometimes dispersed to secondary airfields away from their main base.

In January 1939 the Chief of the Air Staff, Sir Cyril Newall, decided that the RAF should establish daytime decoy airfields using dummy or obsolete aircraft, with a system of lights to be used at night. Tenders were invited for the building of dummy aircraft. By June 1939 it was agreed that a network of decoys would be built east of a line from Southampton through Birmingham to Perth. All permanent main airfields would get a dummy site and every type of airfield would get night lighting decoys.

Alongside this, the Home Office had started work separately on the idea of decoys to protect cities. They carried out an experiment around Hull in May 1939 which involved bathing the entire Humber estuary and surrounding area in light – 4,000 hurricane lamps were laid out on a grid on both sides of the Humber Estuary. It proved impossible for a Whitley bomber flying over the area to distinguish specific targets or towns. However, the idea of bathing virtually the entire country in a similar glow was of course wholly impractical!

A key figure in the decoy story was Colonel John Fisher Turner, an Air Ministry engineer brought out of retirement to co-ordinate the decoy plan. He made a number of modifications to the initial plans, for example, suggesting that the decoys would be more effective if they were further away from the airfields they were protecting. Under Turner's plan they would normally be six miles away rather than just one. Crucially, he brought the expertise of the film industry on board in the form of Norman Loudon of Sound City at Shepperton Studios. His knowledge of building convincing-looking film sets at speed, often with limited resources, was highly relevant

There were many different types of decoy and dummy sites developed to protect airfields, factories and whole cities. It was estimated that 5 per cent of German bombing raids were diverted by these sites. (St Margaret's Richmond)

to the task in hand. In the autumn of 1939, Sound City were contracted to make one hundred Blenheims and fifty Wellington dummies. A number of other film studios were also involved in similar contracts.

Although it is difficult to comprehend this now, the whole of the decoy operation was regarded as top secret. In January 1940 Colonel Turner wrote to the staff at all his decoy sites emphasising the need for secrecy and the importance of not discussing with anyone the nature of the work in which they were engaged. Clearly, the construction of dummy and decoy sites was hardly something that could be done in secret. The end product was intended to be highly visible. However, most of the sites were, by definition, in country areas and, whatever local people knew at the time, there was never any official acknowledgment of the existence of decoys during the war.

There were a number of challenges faced by Turner as he scrambled to get the decoy programme up and running as quickly as possible after the outbreak of war. He faced some difficulty in finding enough suitable sites and Turner found Hugh Dowding, in charge of Fighter Command, to be obstructive. However, eventually, the decoy sites were identified and equipped and came on stream. At the beginning of 1940, twenty-two of the planned thirty-six day decoy sites had been identified and lighting sets had been acquired for most of the fifty planned night time 'Q' sites.

From February 1940 the sites started to become operational. By the time the Battle of Britain started in the summer of 1940, the basic network was in place. 'Q' sites appeared to have an immediate impact. By the end of June 1940, thirty-six bombing attacks were recorded as having been drawn by the decoys away from the sites they were protecting. By the time the Battle of Britain effectively ended in October 1940, it was claimed that seven out of every ten attacks on airfields with night time 'Q' decoys had struck the decoys rather than the real airfields.

As the intensity of Luftwaffe attacks grew in the middle of 1940, there were three important developments of the decoy programme. Firstly, a number of night time sites were identified to the west of the original Southampton – Birmingham – Perth line. Secondly, the idea of creating fires at night time decoy sites, as happened at Lullingstone, was introduced at a number of sites. These became known as 'QF' sites. Thirdly, and perhaps most importantly, the idea was conceived of creating dummy aircraft factories to try to draw enemy bombing away from the real factories. Four factories were initially chosen for dummies – **Short's at Rochester in Kent, De Havilland's at Hatfield, Boulton and Paul's at Wolverhampton and Armstrong Whitworth's at Baginton near Coventry**. In addition, two important wireless stations, at Leighton Buzzard and at Dagnall, were given dummies.

Meanwhile, the idea of protecting whole cities with decoys was still being investigated. In May 1940 the Ministry of Home Security ran two city decoy experiments in Sheffield and Glasgow. Turner and the Air Ministry were angry about this and, after much inter-departmental wrangling, in July 1940 Turner was given overall control of all decoy work in an attempt to ensure better co-ordination. But it was the events of 14 and 15 November 1940 which brought the issue of protecting cities by decoys to a head. The 'Moonlight Sonata' raid on Coventry which cost almost 600 lives (see Chapter One) spurred the development of Starfish sites.

By January 1941 forty-three Starfish sites had been developed protecting fifteen cities and by April 1941, that number had grown dramatically to 130 sites protecting forty-two places. Eventually, a total of eighty-one different places had protection to a greater or lesser extent from a total of 237 Starfish sites. For example, Liverpool, the main port for the Atlantic convoys, had fourteen sites, Glasgow nine, Leeds twelve and London seven. A whole

Sixteen miles to the south-west of Bristol, the Black Down decoy site was designed to create a replica of the city and there are still several remains of the structure visible today. (Rodw)

host of smaller places had just one, including places not necessarily of great industrial or military significance like Guildford, Tunbridge Wells and York.

So by 1941, a complicated and interlocking network of different types of decoy and dummy sites existed across the country. These are some examples:

Black Down, Bristol is one of the few decoy sites in Britain where there are still recognisable remains left in the twenty-first century, and it was one of the most remarkable. Situated about 16 miles south-west of Bristol at the western end of the Mendip Hills, this 'QF' decoy site was based on the idea of creating a fairly accurate replica of the city. It had six specific areas designed to mimic six key areas in the centre of Bristol itself. The lighting pattern created at the decoy site included an attempt to create the impression of a railway marshalling yard and there were even lights that were meant to look like trams. As with other 'QF' sites, if enemy bombers appeared to have been fooled into attacking the decoy site, fires were then lit to give the impression of successful bombing. Two control buildings remain and trenches which were used for setting the fires alight can still be seen at the site.

Sneaton Moor near Scarborough was a 'QF' and Starfish site designed mainly to protect the important industrial facilities of Teesside centred around the city of Middlesbrough about 25 miles to the north. It was operational from June 1941 until some time in 1943. Some remains of the decoy are still visible.

Thorner, near Leeds was one of twelve Starfish sites protecting Leeds. It was also a 'QF' site. Like many such sites it included lighting made to look like a railway marshalling yard, with red and green lights which looked like railway signals as well as real train lamps.

Richmond Park, London. A Starfish site was set up in January 1941, one of seven in and around London to protect the capital. The others were at Rainham Marshes, Lambourne End, Farleigh, Hampstead Heath, Kenn Wood as well as Lullingstone. Ponds on Richmond Park were drained to stop them being a navigational aid. Ditches were dug across the historic parkland to stop enemy aircraft from being able to land there. Like many decoy sites, a heavy anti-aircraft battery was also set up alongside the decoy site.

Banbury Dummy Factory, Banbury, Oxfordshire. The Northern Aluminium Company had established a sheet-rolling factory at Banbury in 1931. Production expanded in the late 1930s to meet demand from the aircraft industry and 4,000 people were working there when the war started. To protect this important industrial plant, the factory was camouflaged and protected by anti-aircraft guns. In addition, though, a dummy factory was built about three miles to the north of the real factory. It stood to the east of the A423 between Great Bourton and Mollington. The decoy was made to look as much like the real factory as possible, complete with a railway siding and smoke coming out of its chimneys. The decoy apparently worked as the real factory was never bombed whereas the decoy was hit in October 1940. The dummy factory was repaired within a week and was never hit again. The dummy buildings were dismantled in the 1960s. The real factory closed in 2009.

Aerial view of the decoy site in Richmond Park in south-west London which was one of seven such sites set up to protect the capital. (St Margaret's Richmond)

At the peak of its activity the decoy and dummy operation masterminded by Colonel Turner occupied almost 800 different sites across Britain with a total of around 1,100 different decoys. However, a network which had been conceived and developed from a virtual standing start at the beginning of the war was to disappear almost as quickly as it had sprung up. From 1943 onwards with the threat from the Luftwaffe lessened, the decoy sites were progressively stood down over the next two years. By the autumn of 1943, the number of Starfish sites had reduced from its peak of 237 down to 144. By the beginning of 1945, there were just sixty-seven occupied decoy sites still in operation representing fewer than 10 per cent of the total.

There were two main reasons for the rundown: the need to save resources and also to divert effort to the deception apparatus needed for D-Day (see

The Alcan Factory at Banbury in Oxfordshire before its closure in 2009. During the war, it was protected by a dummy factory, about three miles to the north, which was hit in an air raid in October 1940 whereas the real factory escaped bombing throughout the war. (Banbury Times)

below). The rapid rundown was also an attempt to try to preserve the secrecy of the decoy operation.

A specific order by the Joint Chiefs of Staff kept a lid on all aspects of the deception war after the conflict had ended. Similar to other post-war bans on discussion of secret aspects of Britain's war effort, this was because of the natural inclination of the British establishment to prefer secrecy. Moreover, there was the quite rational view that the technology and techniques developed during the war might be needed again, particularly as the Cold War started to develop so soon after the Second World War had ended. Indeed, when Colonel Turner died in 1958, his obituary could make no more than a coded reference to the exact nature of his work during the war, stating only that he had been 'specially employed by the Air Ministry'.

By April 1945 the vast network of deception designed to confuse the Luftwaffe had all but disappeared. Just eight decoys remained to protect London and a few others guarding key installations stayed in place elsewhere.

As soon as the war in Europe ended on 8 May 1945 these last few were shut down and dismantled speedily.

So, were the remarkable effort and the considerable amount of resources devoted to decoys worthwhile? In his study of wartime decoys, *Fields of Deception*, Colin Dobinson quotes the Air Ministry claim at the end of the war that 5 per cent of Germany's bombing effort against Britain was diverted by decoy sites with an estimated saving of 2,500 lives. A total of 728 attacks were recorded on decoy sites during the war, 443 of them on night time 'Q' sites and 101 on Starfish sites. A total of twenty-three attacks were recorded on dummy factories. These overall totals may sound modest. However, given that the work to build decoys only really started once the war was underway, it is probably right to say that this was nevertheless a significant achievement.

D-Day Rehearsals and Deceptions

The D-Day landings on 6 June 1944 constitute the largest seaborne invasion in military history. More than 2million service personnel, organised in thirty-nine divisions, 138 battleships, cruisers and destroyers, 287 minesweepers, 310 landings ships, 3,817 landing craft and 10,000 aircraft were involved. British and British Empire forces, American and Canadians made up the bulk of the fighting forces, but many other countries were represented on the armada that crossed the Channel. The operation represented the 'beginning of the end' of the Second World War, as eventually the Allied forces pushed the Germans back from the French coast leading to Germany's eventual surrender the following May.

There were two key ingredients in the build-up to D-Day without which its success might well not have been achieved – deception and preparation. Perhaps the greatest act of deception employed by the Allies during the Second World War was to mislead the Germans about the exact location of the D-Day landings. Operation Fortitude was the codename for the deception which convinced the Germans that the invasion would come via the Straits of Dover to the Pas-de-Calais rather than onto the beaches of Normandy. Another part of the deception was to deceive the Germans into believing that the Normandy invasion, when it did come, was not in fact the main invasion force which would subsequently arrive elsewhere. The fact that the Allies were, at some point, going to launch an invasion was not of course a secret. However, the exact timing and the precise location were crucial facts which the Allies were determined to keep highly confidential so as to maximise the chances of success.

US troops landing on a beach in Devon in April 1944 as part of Exercise Tiger in preparation for the D-Day Normandy landings. (US Library of Congress)

In addition, the extraordinary amount of preparation undertaken before the invasion almost defies belief viewed from the twenty-first century and knowing the outcome. A whole series of rehearsals were held at a variety of locations around Britain to test the invasion plans. In the weeks immediately before the invasion, there was a build-up of people and machines across a vast area of southern England which was unprecedented in scale and complexity.

Among the range of locations associated with the rehearsals, and with the deception operation, were:

South Devon Coast. Slapton Sands, near Torcross in South Devon, was chosen as one of the rehearsal sites for the D-Day landings because of its similarity to what became known as Utah Beach in Normandy – one of the proposed landing beaches for American troops. It has a long straight thin beach with a lake behind. The area around Slapton Sands was forcibly evacuated in late 1943 so that preparations could start. A range of exercises took place, but it was in the last week of April 1944 that a terrible error occurred with the result that Slapton Sands will forever now be associated with one of the most infamous tragedies of the Second World War.

On the morning of 28 April, the rehearsal, codenamed Exercise Tiger, was due to culminate in a mock landing by 30,000 troops on the beach at Slapton. Two things went wrong. German motor torpedo boats, known as E-boats, spotted the ships involved in the exercise and opened fire in Lyme Bay. Worse still, it had been decided that the troops landing on the beach should experience as near as possible real battle conditions by coming under fire from both naval artillery and from the shore. For reasons never adequately explained, live ammunition, as opposed to dummy bullets, was used and many died as a result of this 'friendly fire'.

The total number of deaths was at least 800, mostly Americans, and the survivors of the incident were sworn to secrecy. The casualty numbers were not released at the time of the incident but included in the overall Normandy invasion figures announced in August 1944. It is believed that many of those who died were buried in hastily made mass graves behind the beach at Slapton. Ten senior officers who had high level security clearance in connection with the invasion plans were killed in the incident. It was only when all ten bodies had been recovered that Allied commanders felt they could continue with the plans. Had any of the ten been captured alive, the security of the D-Day operation might have been compromised.

Like so many Second World War secret stories, the disaster of Exercise Tiger was hardly spoken about for many years. Local resident Ken Small recovered a submerged American tank lost in the incident and raised it from the sea. The tank is now part of a memorial next to the beach to those lost in the incident.

North Devon Coast. Several North Devon beaches were also used in D-Day preparations. Woolacombe Beach, Braunton Borrows and Putsborough Sands were among those parts of the coastline used for simulating landing on the Normandy beaches. Amphibious craft were tested and obstacles built on the beaches to try to make conditions as realistic as possible. Defences resembling the Atlantic Wall fortifications, built by the Germans along the French coast, were constructed on these Devon beaches. Live ammunition was used in the exercises here and there were casualties. In 2009, long-forgotten film came to light of the exercises on the North Devon beaches.

A Sherman tank, raised from the seabed in 1984, which now forms a memorial near the beach at Slapton Sands to those who died in the disastrous D-Day rehearsal on April 1944. More than 800 died, some of them by 'friendly fire'. (Shahirshamsir)

Some of this film had been used in newsreels after D-Day purporting to be film from the Normandy beaches themselves. Real footage taken in Normandy was often considered to be too harrowing.

Around 100,000 US troops were stationed in Devon in the months leading up to D-Day. Many holiday camps were requisitioned, but new temporary camps and facilities were also built to house the troops, one of which was Fremington Camp near Barnstaple. A US military hospital with room for 2,000 patients, it received thousands of wounded American service personnel after D-Day.

Pembrokeshire Coast. In August 1943 Operation Jantzen was launched on the beaches of Pembrokeshire as part of the D-Day preparations. The beaches there, around Saundersfoot Bay, were also deemed to be similar to the real

Normandy beaches. A major simulated invasion, involving 100,000 troops, took place there with landing craft, amphibious vehicles and troopships.

The weather was bad and there were many problems with the mock invasion, including a number of submerged craft. Winston Churchill and senior military commanders visited the area one day during the exercise to observe the rehearsals. For many years, a letter from Churchill thanking the landlord for his hospitality hung on the walls of the Wiseman's Bridge Inn near where the exercise took place.

Dorset Coast. Studland in Dorset was the scene of Exercise Smash held on 18 April 1944 and witnessed by Churchill and Eisenhower. This was one of the final rehearsal exercises held near Poole. Live ammunition was used and this exercise was also notable for things that went wrong. It was used to test out a new type of tank, the DD (Duplex Drive) Valentine which was designed to be able to leave its landing craft further out at sea. However, the exercise demonstrated that they did not work as well as expected and six men lost their lives during the trials. As a result, plans for D-Day were modified.

Remains of landing craft lost during D-Day rehearsals conducted on the Pembrokeshire coast in Wales in April 1944. (Unknown)

Gullane Beaches, Scotland. An extensive section of the East Lothian coast, east of Edinburgh, was cordoned off for D-Day rehearsals stretching from Prestonpans in the west to Dunbar in the east. The beach at Gullane was chosen to practise landings because its sand was the same as those of the intended landing beaches in France. Naval frogmen had gone on night time missions to the French coast to take samples. Three weeks of practice landings took place at Gullane in the spring of 1944.

Imber Evacuation. Preparations for D-Day involved the mass evacuation of civilians from inland areas as well as from stretches of coastline. One of the most dramatic of these was the clearing of the Wiltshire village of Imber. On 1 November 1943, the villagers were summoned to a meeting and given forty-seven days to vacate their homes. Allied commanders wanted to use the village as an area for American troops to practise street fighting in advance of D-Day. They wanted Imber to be used to simulate a typical French town. The village, on Salisbury Plain, was in the middle of an area already given over to military activity and the 150 or so villagers told to leave apparently put up little resistance. They were told that they would eventually be able to return, but Imber continued to be used for street fighting training after the war and remains a military area to this day. The villagers were never able to return, although there is public access allowed to the village on a number of days each year.

Tyneham Evacuation. The inhabitants of the Dorset village of Tyneham received a similar summons to those of Imber on 17 November 1943. Here 225 residents were given a month to leave. The letter said, 'The Government appreciates that this is no small sacrifice which you are asked to make, but they are sure that you will give this further help towards winning the war with a good heart.' Like Imber, there was a promise of an eventual return, but it never happened. There were protests after the war but eventually the land was compulsorily purchased. Today it remains part of the restricted Lulworth Ranges area and is generally closed to public access except on certain days.

Final D-Day Build-up – Real and Dummy

There were many aspects to the deceptions around the D-Day landings and a number of locations around Britain played a part in them.

Operation Cockade was an attempt to fool the Germans into believing that the invasion was happening in 1943. It consisted of three elements – a spoof cross-Channel landing which was codenamed 'Starkey', a series of activities giving the impression of a landing in Norway (codenamed 'Tindall'), and a similar set of ruses suggesting an American invasion of Brittany (codenamed 'Wadham').

Colonel Turner's team created a force of dummy Boston aircraft at three Scottish locations – Fordoun, Peterhead and Fraserburgh in August 1943. Dummy aircraft were deployed at ten airfields in southern England as well as thirty-three lighting decoys on the south coast stretching from Portsmouth to Dover. In addition, dummy landing craft were deployed at various points on the south coast to simulate the build-up of an invasion force. There were two types of dummy craft, 'Bigbobs' made of canvas on a steel frame and smaller 'Wetbobs' made of inflatable rubber. A total of 175 of these dummy craft, mixed with some real landing craft, were assembled between Falmouth and Rye. Movements of these craft and the use of false radio signals were all intended to give the impression of an imminent invasion. Then on 9 September 1943, a 'spoof' invasion, using real craft and supported by air cover, set off towards the French coast, coming to a halt 10

Imber Village on Salisbury Plain in Wiltshire remains a restricted area for military training in the twenty-first century more than seventy-five years after its inhabitants were ordered to leave in 1943 to allow D-Day training to take place there. (Scott Wylie)

The abandoned village of Tyneham in Dorset where, on 17 November 1943, 225 residents were given a month to leave before the area was requisitioned. (Nick MacNeill)

miles off Boulogne. However, the Germans were not fooled and no shots were fired. The convoy turned tail and the overall conclusion was that this rather elaborate deception operation had failed.

Nevertheless, similar deception operations were again employed in the build up to D-Day itself in 1944. In the two months up to the invasion, Turner's team created a series of decoys along the south coast. These were designed both to provide protection for the real forces being amassed for the invasion, but also to simulate dummy build-ups of forces with the intention of giving a misleading impression of where the invasion would come. Broadly speaking, there were a series of decoys between Cornwall and Sussex protecting the real troop build-ups. Along the Essex and Suffolk coasts, lighting was purely deceptive and in between, from East Sussex and round the Kent coast, there was a mixture of the two.

Dummy landing craft were built to be placed at various ports and harbours along the English coast in the build-up to D-Day in 1944 as part of an elaborate plan to deceive the Germans about where and when the invasion of mainland Europe would take place. (Imperial War Museum)

Meanwhile, dummy aircraft were once again assembled in Scotland in April 1944, suggesting an attack on Norway, and crucially, from 20 May, the first of what became a dummy force of 255 aircraft was positioned at Yarmouth, Lowestoft, on the Orwell and Deben rivers and at Dover and Folkestone. It is open to question what exact contribution all this deception made to the success of the D-Day invasion. The Germans were fooled into believing that the Normandy assaults were not the main action and crucially failed to divert reserves there, believing that the real invasion would come later via the Pas-de-Calais. However, the false information supplied by double agents may have had more to do with this than the deception methods on the ground around the British coast.

The final aspect of the D-Day story to mention is the transformation that took place of vast areas of southern Britain in order to accommodate the build-up of troops and equipment prior to 6 June 1944. The main concentrations of front-line troops for the first wave of attack were gathered in four main areas – in Sussex, around Portsmouth, in and behind Southampton and in Dorset. But there were many other areas used as well including South Devon, Cornwall, parts of Somerset, two areas of South Wales, Wiltshire, Surrey and some areas north of London. Specific divisions were housed in staging posts known as 'sausages' where security was tight. The areas were guarded by military police and no one was allowed in or out unless there were exceptional circumstances.

In addition, large parts of southern England, including a 10-mile belt inland from the coastline, became a restricted area with no civilians allowed to enter and those living within the zones forbidden to leave. A number of the temporary camps used for the D-Day assembling were subsequently used as prisoner of war camps as captured Germans were sent to Britain for incarceration when the Allied forces advanced across France and into Germany in the months after D-Day. Twenty airbases across southern England were used for the airborne forces which would protect the ground troops involved in the invasion. Two floating harbours, known as Mulberry Harbours, were towed across the Channel and then used as temporary harbours for supplying the forces after the invasion.

When the time came for the invasion, the massive concentrations of troops and equipment moved from their 'sausages' towards the various embarkation ports in what was surely one of the largest mass movements of people ever seen in the UK. Virtually no other traffic was able to use the roads of large parts of southern England during this period. Ports used for the embarkation included Plymouth, Torquay, Weymouth, Bournemouth, Southampton, and Eastbourne. The whole transportation to the ports took five days. It was only at the very last moment that the vast majority of personnel involved were told exactly where they were going. The D-Day armada, originally scheduled to set sail on 5 June, was delayed by twenty-four hours because of the weather conditions.

Overall, the success of the D-Day landings owed something to the deception tactics involved. However, perhaps the most striking conclusion to be drawn from looking at the build-up, is the immense scope and attention to detail of the preparations. This was a mobilisation of people and resources on a quite unprecedented scale. The fact of the imminent invasion was obviously known but the details of timing and location did remain secret.

Chapter Six

Retreats, Reserves and Resistance

The Paddock; Retreats for the Royals and Government; Storing Art Treasures;
Stockpiling Food; Shelters from Bombing; Resistance Bunkers for Last Ditch Stand.

The Paddock, Dollis Hill, London – Churchill's Alternative War Room

On a chilly January evening in 2018, I made my way through a maze of respectable but unremarkable suburban roads to arrive at one of the most fascinating of all Second World War sites in Britain. Here in a quiet, ordinary street in north-west London, a top-secret wartime bunker is to be found. This relic is not buried deep in the countryside or in some other remote location but hidden 12 metres below Brook Road in Dollis Hill, a very ordinary residential street in the heart of London's commuter land. At face value it is a marvellously incongruous setting for such an important wartime facility.

Construction of The Paddock as a reserve Cabinet War Room started in 1939. When it was completed in June 1940, it had cost around £250,000 (around £12million at 2018 values). What had been created below this nondescript street was virtually a replica of the much more famous Cabinet War Room by then in operation below Whitehall in central London. It had been decided that a replacement was needed for the nerve centre of Britain's wartime command network in case bombing forced the country's leaders out of central London.

The choice of location was almost certainly down to three factors.

Firstly, The Paddock was built below the Post Office Research and Development Station and this gave it some anonymity. It is said that, at the time of construction, local people just assumed that this was some sort of development of the Post Office's buildings. It is yet another example of a secret wartime facility 'hidden in plain sight'.

Secondly, this alternative Cabinet War Room was part of a bigger plan to provide emergency command centres for Britain's wartime leaders

The Paddock was built as alternative Cabinet War Rooms in Dollis Hill in north-west London in case the Whitehall Cabinet War Rooms were taken out of action by bombing. It was part of a wider plan to relocate government ministers, MPs and peers and civil servants to the area if the need arose. (Colin Philpott)

in north-west London. Similar facilities were also built close by for the Admiralty which was codenamed Oxgate below the Admiralty chart room in Oxgate Lane, Cricklewood. Likewise, the Air Ministry's underground reserve citadel, known as Station Z was built below the Stationery Office annexe in Harrow.

Thirdly, as with Oxgate, Station Z and many other important wartime government facilities, they were deliberately chosen to be both near the centre of London, but on what was believed to be the safer northern side of the capital.

The buildings under which The Paddock was constructed were themselves an important wartime location. It was at the Post Office Research and Development Station that engineer Tommy Flowers designed and built the Colossus computer which was used during the latter stages of the war at Bletchley Park (See Chapter Three) to crack German codes.

There are occasional public tours of this bunker. Access now, as it was during the war, is through an innocuous-looking door concealed in what was apparently a new Post Office building at street level, from which you descend by stairs to two underground levels. The facility floods regularly and there was plenty of water underfoot as we made our way round the abandoned rooms and spaces of this subterranean world. Even though it has had some other post-war uses, the bunker now looks pretty much as it must have done when it was abandoned in 1944.

Generators, boilers and the remains of the telephone circuitry, which connected The Paddock to the rest of Britain's wartime command infrastructure, can still be seen. It is easy to make out the map room and the small kitchen area (there was no proper canteen). The rooms where telephone operators would have worked and where the BBC studio was built are also obvious. There are some forty rooms in total. The bunker had an air filtration system to protect it against gas as well as blast walls and doors. Reinforced concrete several metres thick protected the subterranean warren.

Unlike the main Cabinet War Rooms under Whitehall, there was no sleeping accommodation in The Paddock. Instead, the Government requisitioned a newly-built apartment block called Neville's Court just a short distance away. This provided sleeping quarters for people who would work in The Paddock, including a specially strengthened suite for Churchill and his private staff.

However, what makes visiting The Paddock particularly poignant is the knowledge that this elaborate facility, built at considerable expense, was never used in a meaningful way throughout the war. After it was completed in June 1940, it was on permanent standby until 1944. Every day a telephone operator had to be on duty there and take phone calls to establish that communications were working properly. It was powered and kitted out with supplies so that it could have come into service at very short notice. The bunker was guarded twenty-four hours a day throughout its wartime state of readiness.

That day never came, as the War Cabinet and the Joint Chiefs of Staff and others were able to direct the war from under Whitehall without interruption throughout the conflict. However, the Cabinet did meet at The Paddock on 3 October 1940, chaired by Winston Churchill, just to test the

The War Cabinet only met twice at The Paddock in October 1940 and in March 1941 and the facility was abandoned before the end of the war. (Colin Philpott)

facilities. It met there once again on 10 March 1941, but without Churchill present. The meeting was chaired by Churchill's deputy, the Labour leader, Clement Attlee, and was also attended by the Australian Prime Minister, Robert Menzies.

Churchill disliked The Paddock describing it as 'a piece of useless folly'. This view was partly attributable to his general antagonism towards any idea that the country's leaders might move away from the traditional heart of British Government in Whitehall and Westminster. In addition, he simply disliked the place and its location. He would not therefore have been disappointed when, in the autumn of 1943, The Paddock was taken out of commission and was replaced by the new emergency war room, codenamed Anson (see Chapter Two), built under Whitehall. The Paddock was finally vacated and cleared in late 1944.

After the war, the bunker lay abandoned and forgotten until the 1960s when the Post Office took over part of it for use as a social club for its staff.

Throughout the war, a telephone operator was on duty every day and tested the communications to ensure that The Paddock could be brought into service at very short notice. (Colin Philpott)

It was considered as a possible Cold War military control room, but rejected for this role because of the problem of flooding. In 1976 the Post Office finally vacated the buildings above. Cadbury Schweppes used the above ground buildings for several years.

In 1997 the site was bought by Network Homes who have redeveloped the site for housing, partly using the existing buildings and partly with newly-built homes. The names Chartwell Court and Tommy Flowers Close bear witness to the wartime heritage of the area. One of the conditions of the planning permission for the development was that public access to the bunker should be maintained, with tours organised twice a year.

Walking below ground in this abandoned relic reminds you of the extraordinary lengths to which wartime planning went to provide back-up facilities, with pretty much no regard to the cost. However, the overriding image I was left with after visiting The Paddock was that of the telephone operator visiting each day during the war to maintain a lonely vigil just in case.

Willesden College, Willesden, London – an Alternative Parliament

As well as the potential relocation of crucial command centres to north-west London, plans had been drawn up for Parliament to move to the same area in the event of severe bomb damage to the Houses of Parliament. In September 1938 the Speaker of the House of Commons approved a plan to relocate the Commons to the Willesden Technical College in Denzil Road, Willesden. The college had a large hall suitable for Parliamentary sessions as well as many other smaller rooms suitable for offices. Under the same plan, the House of Lords would have been relocated to Dudden Hill County School opposite the college. Later, Gladstone Park School was identified as a more suitable location for the Lords.

When war broke out on 3 September 1939, the college was requisitioned and work was undertaken to make it ready for possible occupation by MPs. After the Cabinet held a test meeting at The Paddock in October 1940, there was talk of undertaking a similar rehearsal at Willesden College. This never happened and in fact by then the idea of relocating to Willesden had gone out of favour and potential retreats further afield were being sought. Perhaps this was just as well because, on the night of 10 November 1940, bombs fell in the vicinity of Willesden College killing nine people and seriously damaging the college building.

Willesden College is now part of the College of North West London.

Royal Retreat – Madresfield Court, Near Malvern, Worcestershire

If Government and Parliament had needed to move to Willesden, it would have been because the main Cabinet War Rooms were taken out of action through bombing. However, contingency plans had also been drawn up before the war, for bolt holes well away from London for Royalty and Government in the event of a German invasion.

For King George VI and his family, the royal retreat would have taken them to Worcestershire. Madresfield Court, near Malvern, had been identified in 1938 as part of a wider plan for relocating the machinery of government away from London in the event of invasion.

Madresfield remains the home of the Lygon family today as it has been for almost 600 years. The current house dates from the sixteenth century

The Paddock was built underneath the Post Office Research and Development Station and, after the war, it had several different uses before the whole site was converted into apartments. A condition of the planning consent was the preservation of the bunker. (Barbara Jacob)

but was altered significantly during Victorian times. Evelyn Waugh was a frequent visitor to Madresfield and his novel *Brideshead Revisited* is said to have been inspired by the house and the Lygon family.

The royal evacuation plan would have involved taking the young princesses Elizabeth and Margaret to Madresfield first along with part of the royal retinue, followed later by the king and queen. Food supplies were stocked in the cellars at the outbreak of war. Local businesses were selected to provide food and other essentials, had the plan been implemented, and many local people were required to sign the Official Secrets Act. It is believed that, in the last resort, the royal family would have been guarded at Madresfield by auxiliary units, the British Resistance (see below).

Madresfield's choice as a royal wartime retreat was influenced by several factors. It is a long way from the sea and was close to the proposed defensive line from which a last-ditch resistance to invasion would have been mounted.

Madresfield would have served as a staging post for the royals in the event of a successful invasion by the Nazis. From there the king would have

The Worcestershire country house, Madresfield Court, was earmarked as a retreat for the Royal Family if they needed to leave London during the war – a facet of wartime planning that remained secret until the release of documents in 2006. (Philip Halling)

tried to rally the nation against the invaders, using the nearby BBC studios at Evesham. However, had the invaders secured their grip on London and the south-east, the royal family would have fled further north and eventually sailed for exile in Canada.

The plans for a royal retreat in the Malvern Hills remained unknown to the general public until the release of previously classified documents by the National Archives in 2006.

Stratford-upon-Avon, Warwickshire – Parliament Outside London

The Madresfield plan was part of a wider evacuation scheme for de-camping the machinery of government to the Midlands in the event of invasion or severe dislocation in London. Secret plans were also drawn up to move Government and Parliament to the same area. The Royal Shakespeare Theatre had opened in 1932 in the bard's birthplace of Stratford-upon-Avon. It was built on the site of the original Shakespeare Memorial Theatre, destroyed by fire in 1926. Under the wartime relocation plans, the theatre would have been used to accommodate both Houses of Parliament. The Commons would have met in the main auditorium and the Lords in the Conference Hall.

As part of these plans, a number of other locations in Stratford-upon-Avon were identified to provide office and living accommodation for MPs, peers and their staff. Hotels and private houses were chosen and put on standby. Stratford-upon-Avon was codenamed 'H.K.' among the small group of government officials involved in the planning of the possible move. It is believed that only a proportion of both MPs and peers would have made the move.

Several other locations in Warwickshire and Worcestershire were also involved in this wider government relocation plan. **Hindlip Hall, near Worcester** would have housed various Cabinet-level Ministers and the Prime Minister and staff would have stayed at **Spetchley Park, also near Worcester.**

Plans were drawn up to relocate Government out of London altogether including taking both the House of Commons and the House of Lords to Stratford-upon-Avon where the new Royal Shakespeare Theatre, opened in 1932, would have served as temporary Houses of Parliament. (Unknown)

All these plans remained just that. The German invasion, of course, never came. The Cabinet War Rooms under Whitehall were never breached. However, the Houses of Parliament were damaged by bombing, but Churchill's reluctance to move away from the traditional seat of government power once again came to the fore. Parliament moved neither to Willesden nor to Stratford-upon-Avon but stayed in Westminster, using Church House, right next door to the Houses of Parliament, for some wartime sessions.

The Wilderness Bunker, Tunbridge Wells, Kent

One more location prepared for wartime eventualities, but never apparently used in earnest, was buried beneath woodland just outside Tunbridge Wells. In 1940 and 1941 a network of tunnels was excavated

Remains of a Second World War bunker at Broadwater Down near Tunbridge Wells. The precise reason for its construction in 1940-41 was the subject of much local speculation including the idea that it was one of a series of last redoubts in the event of a German invasion. (Martin Mullins)

below Broadwater Down. The complex created below ground was apparently known as The Wilderness and the widespread local rumour was that it was built as an underground command post for Lieutenant General (later Field Marshal) Montgomery. It was said that the complex had been prepared as one of a series of redoubts for the defence of Britain in the event of a German invasion. Montgomery had a headquarters in Tunbridge Wells but, after the war, he denied that the underground complex had anything to do with him. It is believed that the complex was used for a while during the D-Day landings as a communications centre by the Royal Corps of Signals. What its intended original purpose was remains a mystery.

Ditchley, near Charlbury, Oxfordshire

So much for places of retreat which might have been needed but weren't. Now to a place that was brought into wartime use. Winston Churchill will be forever associated with his country home of Chartwell, near Westerham in Kent. He bought the house in 1922 and it remained his favourite place until shortly before his death in 1965. In the popular mind it was to Chartwell that Churchill retreated during the dark days of war to find solace.

However, he hardly ever went there during his wartime premiership because it was considered a high-risk bombing target. It was south of London and right on the regular flightpath of German bombers en route to and from the capital. Likewise, the Prime Minister's official residence, Chequers, near Princes Risborough in Buckinghamshire, which was very visible with an easily identifiable drive and poor tree cover, was also thought to be vulnerable.

As a result Churchill was offered the use of Ditchley in Oxfordshire, a country house built in 1722 and bought by a Conservative MP, Ronald Tree, who was a pre-war friend of the Prime Minister. Churchill had visited Ditchley many times before 1939 because Ronald Tree was part of a group of anti-appeasement politicians, led by Churchill, who were warning of the threat from Nazi Germany during the 1930s. Ditchley had significant tree cover, a disguised entrance driveway and could not easily be identified from the air.

Churchill used Ditchley between late 1940 and 1943. After this Chequers was considered safe again with the threat from the Luftwaffe reduced and proper camouflaging in place.

Ditchley House in Oxfordshire served as Winston Churchill's country home for much of the war as Chequers, the official country residence of the Prime Minister, was considered vulnerable to bombing. (Jeff Jarvis)

A number of government departments were relocated out of London during the Second World War to safer places. The Air Ministry and Ministry of Aircraft Production had offices in Harrogate, taking over a number of hotels in the North Yorkshire spa town. Other departments went to Cheltenham and Bath.

Art Treasure Stores

The Second World War was a truly existential struggle in which Britain was fighting for its very survival. Given this, worrying about what happened to the nation's art treasures and cultural artefacts might not have seemed like a high priority. However, a great deal of pre-war planning went into securing the safe keeping of Britain's art and much effort was expended on the issue once the war was underway. Apart from the intrinsic need for a civilised society to do this even in times of extreme danger, there was also another motive – a contribution to morale. Damage to, or loss of, national cultural assets would have been seen as highly detrimental to the values of civilisation which Britain and its Allies were fighting to protect.

As early as July 1933, the first meeting took place of a newly-formed Museums and Galleries Air Raid Precautions Committee. Like much pre-war planning for the threat of mass aerial bombardment expected to be a feature of any future conflict, the assumption was that London and its surrounds would be the only target. Therefore, the first strategy of the museum and gallery planners was to look for safe stores for their artefacts well away from the capital.

A list of fifty country houses in various parts of the country was drawn up and owners were contacted to get them to agree to house the art treasures of London's great national museums. It was said at the time that many of them may not have had entirely altruistic motives in agreeing to help the war effort in this way. Most stately homes across Britain were pressed into wartime service in one way or another, often to accommodate evacuees or to billet troops. Faced with that prospect, the idea of storing artworks may have seemed an attractive alternative.

Stately homes away from London were first considered to be safe places to store the nation's art treasures until it became apparent that the Luftwaffe's bombers would be able to reach large parts of the country. Montacute House in Somerset stored material from the V&A. (Becks)

By the time of the outbreak of war in September 1939, the list of allocations of country houses to specific museums had been finalised. These included taking the treasures of the National Gallery to the **University of Wales at Bangor** and the **National Library of Wales at Aberystwyth** as well as a number of other Welsh locations; the British Museum to **Boughton House and Drayton House in Northamptonshire**; the Victoria and Albert Museum to **Montacute House in Somerset**; the Tate to **Muncaster Castle in Cumbria, Hellens at Much Marcle in Herefordshire** and **Eastington Hall in Worcestershire**; the Natural History Museum to **Tring Park in Hertfordshire** and the Science Museum to **Herriand Park and Rutherford Park, both in Hampshire.**

Alongside these plans, the London-based national museums also took steps to safeguard their collections in London. Museum cellars and basements were strengthened to protect against bombing and several Tube lines were made available for the storage of works of art and museum artefacts. A disused subway at Piccadilly Circus Underground Station was used and, most notably, the Aldwych branch of the Piccadilly Line. Train services on the short spur from Holborn to Aldwych were suspended in September 1940. A number of British Museum artefacts and artworks were transported there, including the controversial Elgin Marbles. Material from the British Museum library and some oriental antiquities were also stored there.

The country house scheme did not by and large turn out to be the solution that had been envisaged before the war. Firstly, by the summer of 1940 it had become clear that the bombing threat was not confined to London and the south-east. This had two consequences – that some of the identified 'safe houses' for the nation's art treasures would not in fact be as safe as thought; and that consideration needed to be given to the treasures held in museums outside of London which would also need protection.

In addition, however, a number of issues developed at some of the country estates to which museum collections had been dispersed. Many of the houses were not able to provide proper storage conditions for the priceless treasures in their custody. Environmental conditions were often inadequate with correct temperature and humidity, vital for the safe keeping of many artefacts, sometimes difficult to maintain. There were many rows about the costs of providing the necessary conditions and there were arguments about the incompatibility of storing works of art alongside other activities in the country houses, like the billeting of soldiers.

A number of tunnels on the London Underground system were used to store the treasures of London-based national museums, including those of the British Museum at Aldwych. (ICCROM Archive)

For example, the British Museum's use of two Northamptonshire houses, **Drayton House near Lowick** and **Boughton House near Kettering,** proved problematical. The museum's collection of coins and medals was heaped upon the floor of the kitchen at Boughton House. Other items were stored in an unfinished wing of the house where there was poor ventilation and no heating. Ethnographic items stored in the unheated chapel at Drayton House were growing mildew. The risk of woodworm there was a worry, and there were concerns about whether upper floors could take the weight of the crates of artefacts.

The British Museum's Chief Scientific Officer paid a visit to Drayton House in January 1940 and found the situation very poor. Not only were the climatic storage conditions unsuitable in large parts of the house, but the owner, Major Stopford-Sackville, had been called up and his family had moved out. This meant that the museum staff sent to live in at the house to look after the collection now had to fend for themselves. The Stopford-Sackville's servants, who had previously looked after them, were no longer around. What's more, the museum staff now had the whole house and estate to worry about, including the family's own possessions. Despite the problems, the British Museum's collections stored at Drayton and Boughton remained there until late in 1941 until other solutions were found.

Montacute House near Yeovil in Somerset was the wartime home for some of the Victoria and Albert Museum's most valuable artefacts. These included 120 of the museum's best carpets, 77 tapestries, 5,590 prints and watercolours and a great deal of furniture. Montacute House was an Elizabethan mansion which had been bequeathed to the National Trust earlier in the 1930s. It was in a poor state when the Office of Works negotiated a lease on behalf of the V&A for £450 per year (around £28,000 in 2018 prices).

By 1940 problems had started to appear at Montacute House. Moths got into the tapestries and it was difficult to deal with the problem. Artefacts were for the most part still packed in their transit cases and were closely packed together. Use of the powerful insecticides needed to get rid of the moths risked damaging other artefacts. In addition, there were worries about the fire risks – both from enemy bombers, whose reach was extending to much of the country, but also from the cigarettes of the increasing number of soldiers camped in the grounds. The Long Gallery at Montacute House was considered at particularly high-risk of fire because it was heavily timbered.

Incidentally, the dispersal of the nation's art and artefacts around the country was supposedly a top-secret scheme. Nevertheless, Muriel Clayton, in charge of the V&A's collection at Montacute reported that:

> 'It is true that a great pretence of secrecy has been observed with regard the place to which the nation's treasures have been sent. But I need hardly tell you that everyone in the neighbourhood knows that our stuff is at Montacute, and I have no doubt that the same applies to the country houses that are being used by… other national museums and galleries.'

At other country house repositories up and down the country, similar problems were reported – unsatisfactory storage conditions, difficult relationships between museum staff and owners, rows about money and the conflicts caused by other users of the houses.

Meanwhile, back in London, the use of tube tunnels for storage ran into difficulties. There were two issues. Local authorities in London wanted tube tunnels for public air raid shelters and, after the heavy bombing of London during the Blitz of 1940-1941, there was concern that a direct hit on a tube station would probably damage the tunnels below and endanger the artefacts. The Elgin Marbles remained at the Aldwych, but other art treasure stores on the Underground were generally vacated.

From 1941, the country house storage scheme was formally abandoned although some collections did remain in stately homes until later in the war.

The alternative solution was large underground repositories in remote parts of the country. This was an idea which had been suggested before the war but rejected on grounds of cost. However, throughout 1940 and into early 1941, the idea of finding suitable deep stores was revived. Sir John Forsdyke, of the British Museum, who had long been an advocate of going underground, wrote to the Treasury:

> 'It was recognised long before the war by the Museums and Galleries, and by the Office of Works, that the only safe storage would be underground. Accommodation in Tube Railway stations and tunnels…is satisfactory as far as it goes, but it does not go very far. The kind of material that can be kept there is limited to what is waterproof. The humidity of the tubes is normally too high…. Only one of the (country houses allocated to us) is a strong or fireproof building. Other locations have been made dangerous by the construction of aerodromes or barracks nearby…. They contain in concentrated form the most valuable and the most delicate things that the nation possesses…. It is evident that the perishable things of first-rate importance ought to be put underground.'

In the end, two underground quarries in different parts of the country became the stores for many of Britain's most priceless works of art and other cultural treasures. The first was **Westwood Quarry at Corsham in Wiltshire** which was part of the vast labyrinth of underground wartime facilities in that part of the West Country. The Royal Enfield Company occupied part of the quarry but in March 1941 it was agreed that other parts of the quarry, totalling just under 2,000 square metres would be converted at a cost of £19,500 (about £1million at 2018 values) for museum storage.

The fact that a special underground store was being prepared for the nation's art treasures was not a secret. There was discussion about it in the papers, but the precise location did apparently remain under wraps. The British Museum and the V&A were the main tenants and during the summer of 1942 the two museums organised their deliveries of artefacts to arrive on alternate days. Lorry loads arrived day after day, both

Westwood Quarry, part of the vast underground complex at Corsham, became operational as a store for the treasures of a number of museums in 1942. (ICCROM Archive)

from their London bases and also from the country house repositories they were generally glad to vacate. However, once the wider museum community became aware of the plan, there were many requests for space at Westwood. For example, the Science Museum asked to store Orville Wright's Kittyhawk aeroplane there which was on loan from the United States, a request that was granted. The National Portrait Gallery, the Bodleian Library, the Kenwood Collection and others were all able to make use of the Westwood Quarry.

By the end of 1942, after a number of teething problems with the air conditioning, the Westwood repository was fully up and running. Ironically, of course, by then the threat from the Luftwaffe was much reduced. However, the move to Westwood came too late to save tens of thousands of books lost in the British Museum library in London during an air raid on 10 May 1941.

Some country houses and other locations remained in use for art storage including at **Skipton Castle in North Yorkshire** and at the **University of Aberystwyth**. However, Westwood remained the main place of safety for Britain's art treasures and cultural artefacts until the end of the war. Her Majesty Queen Mary visited on 31 March 1943.

Manod Quarry, Blaenau Ffestiniog, North Wales was the other underground store housing Britain's art treasures. This was developed by the National Gallery independently of other national museums. Prior to the war, the National Gallery had drawn up plans to disperse its pictures to a number of locations. In the final week of August 1939, the plan was put into operation with military precision and the art was sent to the National Library of Wales at Aberystwyth, to Prichard Jones Hall at the University of Bangor and to Penrhyn Castle.

However, like the country houses and other locations used by other museums, similar problems arose with the National Gallery's 'places of safety'. By the middle of 1940, North Wales was no longer immune to the threat of bombing. National Gallery staff sent to look after their collections there reported their fears of Welsh nationalist sentiment being stirred up if the war got more difficult. The problems of proper storage

The National Gallery pursued its own underground storage plan and many of its priceless treasures were taken by rail and road to Manod Quarry near Blaenau Ffestiniog in North Wales. (BRB Residuary Body)

conditions also surfaced and Lord Penrhyn, the owner of Penryhn Castle, proved difficult.

All these problems led to the evacuation of some pictures to other locations in Wales as a temporary measure, but the search was on for an underground solution. On 17 September 1940, the gallery's scientific advisor, Francis Rawlins, working with local civil engineers, discovered an apparently suitable quarry site that could be converted into an underground repository. Manod Quarry at the end of a five-mile track above the village of Blaenau Ffestiniog was a suitably remote location and capable of being converted appropriately. It had natural chambers 30 metres high and heated and air-conditioned 'houses' were built inside the quarry to provide the right conditions. The acquisition of the quarry happened very quickly and less than a year later, on 12 August 1941, it was ready for use. In little over a month 2,000 pictures were transported there by rail and in lorries disguised as food delivery vans. The whole operation was supposedly secret but local people are widely believed to have known what was happening but kept quiet about it.

At the end of the war, the art treasures stored at Westwood, Manod and elsewhere went back to London – swiftly in some cases, more slowly in others. All of the National Gallery's pictures were back in the capital by the end of 1945. The V&A returned their material to London from Westwood starting in June 1945 and completed the task by March 1947. The British Museum artefacts went back to London over a similar period. Some of the items stored in London tube stations remained in their temporary homes longer, including the Elgin Marbles which stayed in the Aldwych tube tunnel until late 1948.

Although, with the benefit of hindsight, the development of Westwood and Manod was too late, overall Britain's most priceless works of art and other cultural icons were well protected. As well as the losses in the bombing of the British Museum in 1941, one significant painting, 'Destruction of the Children of Niobe' by Richard Wilson and in the possession of the Tate Gallery was lost in the war. It was destroyed by fire when it was being restored in a private workshop in London which was hit by bombing. A number of big London museums, including the Tate and the National Gallery suffered significant bomb damage. Museums outside London were also hit. However, given the volumes of art and artefacts, these losses were a very small proportion of the total.

After the war, both Manod and Westwood repositories were kept in case they were needed again to store art treasures in future conflicts.

Around 2,000 pictures from the National Gallery's collection were stored at Manod but they were returned to London very quickly after the end of the war in 1945. (BRB Residuary Body)

However, both facilities were disposed of in the 1980s. Today, Westwood is a private high security document store. Manod has returned to being a working quarry.

Food Dumps

If you take a train on the Leeds to York line via Harrogate, you pass the remains of a station long since closed. The last time you could get off at **Goldsborough Station, near Knaresborough, North Yorkshire** was in 1958. But during the war, this station had an important but secret role in ensuring Britain's survival. The location was deliberately chosen to be near a railway line and also close to the A1 road less than a mile away to the east. The store was built right next to the station and was served by specially built sidings.

Goldsborough was the site of one of forty-three cold stores built during the Second World War for the storage of emergency food supplies. The cold stores were identical and built in 1941 and, with a few exceptions, constructed in areas that were away from parts of the country considered most vulnerable to bombing. An estimated 6.5 million tons of food was held at the stores. A network of grain silos was also built at the same time. This was all part of a contingency plan to handle possible severe food shortages if Britain's lifeline of supplies across the Atlantic was cut.

After the war, the cold stores were kept on as Cold War emergency food centres, but by the 1960s, it was decided that this was no longer necessary. A number of stores, including the one at **Hexham in Northumberland** became Cold War Regional Seats of Government. Some of the stores, like the one at **Farncombe in Surrey**, were demolished. Others, like Goldsborough, were sold off and became private refrigerated stores. The Goldsborough store continued in this role until the early part of the twenty-first century. The original cold store has recently been demolished and the

Remains of ARP Signal Box on the Harrogate to York railway line at what was Goldsborough Station near Knaresborough, the location of one of forty-three emergency food cold stores built during the war. There are now commercial premises on the site. (Colin Philpott)

site is now part of a general distribution depot. The remains of the ARP (Air Raid Precaution) signal box on the site can still be seen.

Public Shelters

One of the defining images of Second World War Britain is that of the fairly rudimentary air raid shelters built in back gardens, so-called Anderson Shelters named after Sir John Anderson, who was in charge of pre-war air raid defence planning. As the war intensified and, with the ferocity of bombardment endured during the Blitz of 1940-41 and beyond, it was recognised that more substantial means of protecting the civilian population from air raids were needed, so the idea of utilising large underground spaces was adopted in many cities around the country:

London Deep Level Shelters. Eight underground shelters, each capable of accommodating 8,000 people, were built in London. They were at **Belsize Park, Camden Town, Chancery Lane, Clapham Common, Clapham North, Clapham South, Goodge Street and Stockwell Underground Stations.** Each had two newly built tunnels, about 120 metres long; two further planned deep level shelters, at St Paul's and the Oval, were abandoned.

The tunnels were built for wartime emergency use but with the idea that, after the war, they might be incorporated into extensions or developments of the underground network, particularly the idea of north-south and east-west express tube lines. Work started in November 1940 but the first shelters weren't ready until March 1942. By the time they were ready, the threat from the Luftwaffe had receded, so they weren't brought into immediate use. Indeed, some of the shelters were given over to other uses. The Goodge Street tunnel became General Eisenhower's HQ and others were used to billet troops.

However, the arrival of the V1 and later V2 rockets over London posed a major new threat and some of the shelters were brought into use as public refuges from July 1944, a role they maintained until the end of the conflict. Immediately after the war, some of the shelters continued to be used by people who had been bombed out of their homes. Goodge Street continued as an army transit centre until 1956 and Chancery Lane became a secret telephone exchange. Clapham South was used in 1948 as temporary accommodation for immigrants from the West Indies who arrived on the *Windrush* ship. Three of the eight shelters were incorporated into later developments of the underground system. The entrances of these shelters are in most cases still visible at street level.

Victoria Tunnel, Newcastle-upon-Tyne. The Victoria Tunnel had been built on the north side of the River Tyne between 1839 and 1842 for a subterranean wagonway transporting coal to be loaded onto barges. It was a short-lived function and from 1860, the tunnel was largely abandoned and forgotten, apart from a brief period in the 1920s as a mushroom farm. However, in 1939 at a cost of £37,000 (roughly £2million at 2018 values), the tunnel was brought back into use as an air raid shelter able to accommodate 5,000 people with bunk beds for 500. There were chemical toilets, and the two-mile tunnel had seven entrances. Since the war, part of the tunnel has

Clapham South, one of eight deep-level public shelters in London built at tube stations with a view to incorporating them into planned improvements to the underground system after the war. (Unknown)

been converted into a sewer but about a third of it has been renovated and is now open as a visitor attraction.

Many other British cities made similar uses of underground facilities for public air raid shelters. These included newly-built **Tranmere Tunnels under Birkenhead in Merseyside,** capable of holding 6,000 people and mainly designed for the strategically important workforce of the Cammell-Laird shipyards. The tunnels were 600 metres long and cost around £130,000 (£7million in 2018); **Chislehurst Caves in London,** containing over 20 miles of tunnels and said to have accommodated over 15,000 one night during the height of the Blitz; the **Manchester Co-op Tunnels** which was a network of tunnels built in the 1920s underneath and connecting the Co-operative Society's headquarters buildings in the centre of Manchester and the basement plant room area of **Smethwick Baths in the West Midlands.**

Originally a tunnel for a wagonway linking coal mines with the River Tyne, the Victoria Tunnel in Newcastle was converted into a public air raid shelter capable of accommodating 5,000 people. (Ouseburn Trust)

Resistance Bunkers

Tragically, **Coleshill House, near Coleshill in Oxfordshire**, an elegant, seventeenth-century country house, almost certainly designed by Inigo Jones, was severely damaged by fire in 1952 and subsequently demolished in 1958. In the latter part of its life, the house played a fascinating role in the story of the Second World War, a story which remained largely secret for many decades after 1945.

Today, only the gate posts of Coleshill remain but the estate, owned by the National Trust, is open to the public from time to time. Visitors to the estate are rewarded with the opportunity to experience first-hand what it must have been like to be part of one of the most shadowy, secretive aspects of the war. Coleshill House was requisitioned to be the headquarters and training centre of the innocuous-sounding Auxiliary Units. These were highly trained cells of four to eight men who were to mount a guerrilla sabotage campaign against German forces in the event of an invasion of Britain. They operated from concealed operational bases in underground bunkers. Since the war, the Auxiliary Units have become known colloquially as the British Resistance although it was not a title used at the time.

At Coleshill, the original bunker is no longer accessible, but a replica has been created. The entrance is via a trap door in the woodland. It is easily visible now, but would have been carefully concealed back in the 1940s. The bunker is reached by a ladder down a vertical shaft which leads to an underground room about 4 metres long. Inside there are bunk beds, a table, a basic toilet, an ammunition store and somewhere to prepare food. There is an escape tunnel at the other end.

There were an estimated 1,000 operational bases like the one at Coleshill around the country serving 635 separate Auxiliary Unit patrols. Some units had more than one base. The patrols extended from Cornwall to Scotland but were concentrated in coastal areas and were more numerous in the areas considered most vulnerable to invasion in the south-east of England.

The idea for the Auxiliary Units had very high-level support. It was set up by Colin Gubbins, who had led British Commandos in Norway in 1939 and 1940. He was asked by Churchill to establish the units and they were under the command of the General Headquarters, Home Forces. Gubbins had previously had experience of undercover fighting in the Russian Civil War and in the Irish War of Independence. He later became the leading light in the Special Operations Executive (see Chapter Two).

Reconstruction of an Auxiliary Unit bunker at Coleshill in Oxfordshire, one of an estimated 1,000 such sites around the country from where the British Resistance would have mounted a guerrilla campaign in the event of a German invasion. (Coleshill Auxiliary Research Team)

The men who became 'Auxiliers' were often local landowners or farmers, usually with very good local knowledge. Some were men in reserved occupations who were unable to be called up to the regular armed forces. Others were recruited directly from the Home Guard which had been established in early 1940 to act as regular local defence volunteers. The normal Home Guard operated openly but the clandestine Auxiliary Units operated under the banner of the Home Guard, a ruse which provided a useful cover for their activities. There were an estimated 5,000 Auxiliers recruited in total.

The Auxiliers, who were all civilians, were intended to be a uniformed guerrilla army. Their training, carried out by regular Army personnel, was designed to equip them with the dark arts of sabotage, unarmed combat, the demolition of bridges, roads and other structures. A critical aspect of the way the units were organised was that they were largely self-contained. They were expected to be self-sufficient. Their life expectancy in the event of invasion was expected to be short, maybe twelve to fourteen days. It is said that they were trained to kill each other or themselves if necessary to avoid capture.

Within the Auxiliary Units, there was also an even more secretive section called the Special Duties Branch. A further 3,000 men and women were recruited to be the 'eyes and ears' on the ground to report back to Army commanders in the event of an invasion. These recruits were specially vetted by intelligence officers to act as spies, reporting any useful intelligence and anything gleaned from 'careless talk'. These spies would leave information in 'dead-letter boxes' from where couriers would convey them to Special Duties Branch Out-Stations. These were concealed wireless stations which would then transmit messages back to In-Stations collating intelligence to help the resistance effort against invading forces.

Auxiliary Units stayed in existence long after the realistic threat of invasion had passed. They were finally disbanded in 1944. Part of the reason for the delay was to preserve their secrecy under cover of the Home Guard. Auxiliary Unit members were under strict instructions not to discuss what they did even with their closest family members. For several thousand people, who were apparently just regular members of the Home Guard, suddenly to have been stood down before the end of the war might have risked lifting the lid on the whole Auxiliary Unit project.

Preserving the secrecy of the Auxiliary Units was a very high priority. Nina Hannaford is part of the organisation CART (The Coleshill Auxiliary Research Team) which researches the history of the units and preserves their memory. She has a family interest in the subject. Her grandfather, two of her uncles and a great uncle were all Auxiliers. She has direct evidence of the seriousness with which the secrecy of the operation was taken. Her grandmother told her long after the war that she had been completely unaware of what her husband and other family members were doing. She believed that they were simply regular members of the Home Guard.

There were some breaches of security. In 2001 a man called David Best revealed in a newspaper article how, as a young boy, he and some friends had stumbled across an Auxiliary Unit operational base at Marldon near Torquay:

Steps leading to the Auxiliary Unit bunker at Coleshill. Entrances to these bunkers were carefully concealed and members of the units operated under the cover of being members of the Home Guard. (Coleshill Auxiliary Research Team)

'Although young…we knew this was important stuff and we had the sense to leave the hardware alone but we do admit to snipping bits of fuse wire which we let off the next day to the cheers of our schoolboy audience'.

When this happened, and Auxiliers knew their bases had been discovered, they abandoned them and found a new location.

A former AU member from the south-west also attested to the lengths to which the units would have gone to preserve the secrecy of operational bases in the event of invasion. He said that the unit he served in had a base at the end of a country lane. An elderly couple living in the lane knew about the base. The former member claimed that, had the invasion happened, the couple would have been killed by Auxiliers as a precaution.

There was also the case of an Auxilier in Somerset who was found to have been saying too much about what he did. He was told his services were no longer required. There are also many testimonies from former Auxiliers that unit leaders were frequently visited by intelligence officers and reminded of the need for secrecy.

After the war, the existence of the Auxiliary Units was briefly made public. Articles in several newspapers immediately after the end of the war made reference to the organisation. The *Western Morning News* described them as the 'British Maquis' referencing the name of the French Resistance groups during the war. Generally, however, the story stayed out of the limelight until the 1990s. Since then many of those who served in the Auxiliary Units have spoken about their experiences.

Very few Auxiliary Unit bunkers are known still to exist but the headquarters of the Eaton unit remains in the Harford Mill, south of Norwich. (Coleshill Auxiliary Research Team)

Most of the operational bases were emptied and destroyed when the Auxiliers were disbanded. However, there are tell-tale remains of these secret bunkers in various parts of the country. For example, in the **Harford Hills, south of Norwich,** the remains of the Eaton Auxiliary Unit operational base can still be seen inside the Danby Wood Nature Reserve. Generally, however, virtually nothing remains of the places where this shadowy organisation operated.

Chapter Seven

Interrogation, Internment and Indiscretions

Interrogation Centres; London Cage, Camp 020 and others; Prisoner of War Camps; Internment Camps; 'Careless Talk' – Treason, Treachery and the Defence Regulations

Context

Bundesarchiv, Bild 183-J28589
Foto: Büschel | 1944/1945 Winter

American troops captured in December 1944 by German forces – Germany, Britain and the United States generally treated each other's prisoners of war in accordance with the Geneva Convention. (Büschel, Bundesarchiv)

Prisoner of war (PoW) camps were not secret during the Second World War. In general, their location was known to the people living nearby. Indeed, many prisoners were involved in their local communities, often working outside the camps. Moreover, the requirements of the Geneva Convention and other international agreements meant that the combatant nations were supposed to inform the International Red Cross of the location of camps. This was to enable representatives of neutral countries and the Red Cross to inspect the camps and to try to ensure that treatment of prisoners was in accordance with international law. Nevertheless, there were a number of aspects of Britain's treatment of PoWs and others that remained highly secretive.

Overall, the British, Americans, and other Allied Powers did abide by the rules governing PoWs. The Germans likewise treated British and American prisoners properly. However, the Germans and Russians treated each other's prisoners badly and the Japanese mistreatment of PoWs is well-chronicled. The rules about prisoners of war which applied during the Second World War had been enshrined in the Geneva Convention of 1929. The Convention had been signed by most of the combatant nations in the war but not by the Soviet Union, nor was it ratified by Japan.

The key requirements of the Convention included: the provision of proper food rations (equivalent to those provided to the host nation's own troops); a ban on being put to work that helped the host's war effort; a ban on inhumane or degrading treatment and a requirement that, if interrogated, PoWs were not obliged to reveal more than their name, rank and serial number.

However, the idea that Britain acted wholly and unequivocally in accordance with the Geneva Convention is seriously open to question. By the end of the war, there were an estimated 340 main PoW camps and 1,200 smaller camps across Britain. The vast majority would appear to have been run properly and humanely. The allegations of dubious methods centre mainly on a few locations used as interrogation centres, including the notorious London Cage and Camp 020, as well as a post-war interrogation centre set up by the British occupying forces in Germany.

As well as interrogation designed to get information about enemy forces and plans, another vital element of wartime control in Britain was the prevention of vital information leaking out in the other direction. Internment of foreign nationals and a whole array of new laws and regulations designed to protect information from 'careless talk' were important wartime weapons. The story of how Britain mobilised buildings and spaces of all types right across the country to achieve all this is a fascinating one.

London Cage, Kensington Palace Gardens, London

The street at the heart of questions about Britain's wartime interrogation techniques sits in one of the most exclusive and fashionable parts of London. Numbers 6 and 7 Kensington Palace Gardens now form part of the Russian Embassy. Numbers 8 and 8a were demolished in the 1960s and replaced by billionaire apartments. Several other foreign embassies and consulates are situated on the street, as well as very expensive private houses. The street is guarded at both ends by police but there is nothing remaining to indicate what happened here in the 1940s.

The requisitioning of houses in Kensington Palace Gardens started in October 1940 and Lieutenant Colonel Alexander Scotland started setting up an interrogation centre there. The first prisoners arrived on 23 October 1940. Eventually there were twenty-eight rooms and the centre could accommodate sixty prisoners at any one time. In 1941 part of the paddock of the neighbouring Kensington Palace itself was also taken over to provide supplementary, tented accommodation.

Kensington Palace Gardens was conceived as one of a network of 'cages' around the country (see below). Their role was to question captured enemy prisoners of war and determine their usefulness for further questioning. The vast majority of Italian and German PoWs stayed only briefly in these holding camps as they were deemed not to have any information useful to the Allied war effort. They were then sent on to regular PoW camps. However, some, generally high-ranking officers, were deemed worthy of further interrogation.

This type of interrogation was carried out by yet another clandestine operation of the British wartime machine, the Combined Services Detailed Interrogation Centre (CSDIC). This organisation had started work in the Tower of London at the beginning of the war. However, the need for more space and a base safe from the bombing risk of central London led CSDIC to establish three bases outside the capital (see below) but the London Cage also acquired a role as a formidable, and later a controversial, interrogation centre.

It is estimated that around 3,000 German prisoners passed through the doors of the London Cage throughout the war. What is clear is that the Cage was never declared by the British authorities as an official PoW

Numbers 8 and 8a, Kensington Palace Gardens, which formed part of the interrogation centre which became known as the London Cage. (Foreign Office)

camp to the Red Cross until 1946. After the war ended, the Cage became an interrogation base for the investigation of German war crimes. What remains unclear is whether the interrogation carried out there both during and after the war was authorised as part of the overall CSDIC operation. Some believe it wasn't and that it was largely a rogue operation pursued in defiance of official policy by its maverick boss, Alexander Scotland.

Scotland was an unusual man. Curiously, he had served in the German Army in the early twentieth century in Southern Africa and also spent time as a German PoW during the First World War. Later in that war, he served in British intelligence. He met Hitler in Munich in 1937 and at the beginning of 1940 he signed up with British intelligence again.

The evidence about the methods employed at the London Cage comes principally from Scotland's own post-war memoirs, but also from the claims of captured Germans when they appeared in war crimes trials in the late 1940s. A number of official files about the existence and operation of the London Cage remain classified; others were apparently lost.

In summary, the allegations concerning the London Cage include claims that undoubtedly involve breaches of the Geneva Convention, even though they are clearly not of the same severity as the treatment meted out by the Japanese, Germans and indeed Russians. Many people might question whether Germans on trial for war crimes can be regarded as entirely reliable witnesses about what happened during their interrogation. However, they alleged that they were doused with cold water, forced to clean rooms with a toothbrush, denied food for long periods, deprived of sleep for several days and made to stand to attention for hours without a break. There were a variety of claims of the use of so-called truth drugs and of extreme psychological pressure put on detainees. Lieutenant Colonel Scotland was himself accused of hitting a number of PoWs.

There were also claims that prisoners at the London Cage were repeatedly threatened with a range of worse treatments including deportation to Russia and even execution. Those official files about the London Cage which have been released into the National Archives make reference to 'secret control gear' and to electric shock treatment. There were at least four suicides reported at the London Cage in the immediate post-war period.

Many of the claims about the London Cage appear to relate to the period after 1945 when interrogation of alleged war criminals was the principal activity there. This might explain, though perhaps not justify, the harsh treatment apparently inflicted upon people interrogated there who ranked among some of the most despicable of men in twentieth-century history. Fritz Knöchlein was an SS lieutenant colonel who faced trial as the alleged leader of the so-called Le Paradis massacre in France in 1940. More than 100 British soldiers, who were in the process of surrendering during the retreat to Dunkirk, were gunned down by an SS division on 27 May 1940.

Knöchlein was held at the London Cage for sixty-four days from October 1946. When his trial took place in Germany in October 1948, he alleged that he had been tortured there. He claimed that he had been given virtually no food for three days and that he had been unable to sleep for a similar period because he had been placed in a room where his guards were singing and playing cards. He said that he was forced to do 100 trunk bends without a break and that he was made to walk round in a narrow circle in the same direction for four hours. When he complained of feeling giddy, he was kicked by the guards. He said he was made to do unnecessary cleaning tasks, that he was refused use of the toilet, forced to stay in cold showers for long periods and made to clean floors kneeling down with a guard sitting on his back.

These claims by Knöchlein led to the remarkable sight of his interrogator, Alexander Scotland, ending up in the dock defending himself against war crimes. Scotland fiercely denied Knöchlein's testimony and the court came to no firm conclusion about the truth of the allegations. It ruled instead that the claims were irrelevant to the question of the SS officer's guilt. Fritz Knöchlein was convicted for his part in the Le Paradis massacre and sentenced to death. He was hanged on 21 January 1949.

Although the allegations against Scotland were left unproven, his court appearance left an air of controversy around the London Cage which had finally closed in autumn 1948. Scotland tried to get permission to publish his memoirs in 1954 but was refused on the grounds that their publication would breach the Official Secrets Act. His book came out in 1957 but was heavily redacted. Scotland maintained until his death in 1965 that he had not used torture at the London Cage although he admitted to creating a harsh environment, believing that to be justifiable and necessary to deal with hardened Nazis and, in many cases, war criminals.

Other 'Cages'

The London Cage was effectively the headquarters of a network of cages set up around the country for the initial interrogation of prisoners of war captured by British forces. Many of these were pretty rudimentary affairs, generally tented accommodation, often using requisitioned sports grounds. These 'cages' were under the overall command of Lieutenant Colonel Scotland who is known to have visited them frequently and to have conducted investigations himself at a number of them.

In the first two years of the war, the numbers of PoWs were relatively low. There had been few Allied victories and therefore few enemy combatants taken prisoner. In addition, there was a policy at first of trying to ship PoWs away from Britain to other parts of its Empire, including Canada. There was a fear that groups of enemy PoWs might pose a threat in the event of a German invasion. However, as the war went on, the numbers increased markedly to a peak after the D-Day landings in 1944.

There is some confusion about classification and therefore which camps were regarded as 'cages' at the time but it is generally accepted that there were eleven around the country:

'Deepdale' Preston North End Football Ground, Preston, Lancashire. Preston North End received £255 a year (about £10,000 in 2018 values) from the War Office for the use of their ground and car park during the war. The whole ground was requisitioned in 1940 and the club was unable to use any of the facilities for several years. The Pavilion Stand was used to hold prisoners of war who were allowed to exercise on the pitch. A cookhouse was erected in 1943.

Kempton Park Racecourse, Sunbury-on-Thames, and Lingfield Park Racecourse, Lingfield, both in Surrey. These two Surrey racecourses were the principal 'cages' used to process PoWs arriving via the ports in the south of England – 33,000 PoWs are believed to have passed through Kempton Park. Kempton and Lingfield were also used to house German and Italian nationals interned under the defence regulations.

Several other racecourses in other parts of the country were also used as 'cages' including: **Ascot Racecourse, Sunningdale, Berkshire; Doncaster Racecourse, South Yorkshire; Catterick Racecourse, North Yorkshire and Newmarket Racecourse, Newmarket, Suffolk.**

Dunstable Downs, Dunstable, Bedfordshire was the location of another 'cage'. It was opened in 1940 on the site of what is now the London Gliding Club.

Colchester Cage, Colchester, Essex was an important centre for PoWs. As well as a main PoW camp housing 6,000 prisoners at Berechurch Hall, the Colchester Cage is believed to have been located in the grounds of Achnacone, a large house near Braiswick on the north side of the town. The site of the 'cage' is now a housing development. There is still a military presence at Berechurch Hall where the Military Corrective Training Centre, a prison and rehabilitation centre for members of all the armed services, are located.

There were also 'cages' in **Swindon and Edinburgh.**

Camp 020, Latchmere House, Ham Common, London

Camp 020 at Latchmere House in the leafy south-west suburbs of London is yet another example of a wartime location of great strategic significance nestling in an innocuous-looking backwater. Camp 020 was not designated

Latchmere House in South-West London pictured in 2011 before the site's redevelopment for housing. During the war it was Camp 020 used for interrogating and 'turning' German agents. (Ken Bailey)

as a PoW camp because it was where British intelligence, in the form of MI19, interrogated captured spies and agents. Spies were not armed combatants and were therefore not protected by the Geneva Convention. However, Latchmere House continues, like the London Cage, to be dogged by allegations of brutal treatment and torture.

The centre played a crucial role in extracting information of strategic importance from enemy agents. Above all, it was one of the places where captured agents were 'turned' and became double agents working for British intelligence. Britain's record at capturing and turning German spies was remarkable. There appear to have been very few cases of German spies evading capture for long once they arrived in Britain. In addition, a very high proportion of them were successfully recruited to switch sides and work for the Allies. This was of crucial importance in many aspects of the conduct of the war, particularly around the successful deception achieved with regard to the precise location and timing of the D-Day landings.

Latchmere House was run by Lieutenant Colonel Robin 'Tin-Eye' Stephens who vigorously denied that torture had been employed there. His view, echoed by many other British Second World War interrogators, was that torture seldom produces accurate information. It often leads the prisoner to say what they think the interrogator wants to hear, whereas information cajoled by peaceful persuasion is much more likely to be reliable. Despite that, the regime adopted by Stephens at Camp 020 was formal and forbidding. Interviews were conducted without any pretence of friendship between questioner and questioned. Prisoners had to stand to attention throughout. Stephens was by all accounts severe, bad-tempered and highly xenophobic.

Perhaps most importantly, Camp 020 employed two methods which were very successful in getting high quality information out of captured spies and agents. They used 'stool-pigeons', cellmates in whom agents would confide. The captured agents believed they were fellow agents, but they were in fact either double agents or fake prisoners working with the interrogators. Most importantly, prisoners' cells were bugged to record their unguarded comments. Listeners were sitting in so-called 'M' Rooms eavesdropping on these conversations, a tactic which produced much valuable information. This might sound a fairly obvious tactic to us today, but it was technologically and politically quite an innovation back in the 1940s.

A total of 480 prisoners of thirty-four nationalities passed through Camp 020 including British Fascists. Fourteen were shot for treason or treachery and fifty-five found innocent, but most were either convicted and imprisoned or later freed in return for co-operation.

According to Ian Cobain, who has studied the history of British interrogation before, during and since the Second World War, a number of unsavoury practices took place at Camp 020. These included sleep deprivation, mock executions, leaving inmates naked for long periods and a range of other forms of psychological and mental torture. Physical torture and beatings were, it seems, generally avoided because they were thought to be ineffective and because they left evidence.

Stephens' reputation arises not so much from what happened at Camp 020 during the war but in Germany after the war. He was put in charge of a British interrogation camp at Bad Nenndorf in Lower Saxony which was set up to hold and question suspected Nazi war criminals. It operated for two years from the summer of 1945. Allegations of serious brutality and maltreatment of prisoners there led to a court-martial appearance for Stephens. He was charged with four counts of conduct prejudicial to good order and military discipline, failure in his duty as a supervisor of the camp, and two counts of disgraceful conduct of a cruel kind. Three other officers were also court-martialled. The proceedings were held in secret, Stephens was acquitted and the camp doctor, Captain John Smith, was the only one found guilty.

During his court-martial, Stephens refuted all the allegations of physical violence and torture levelled against him. He maintained that both at Bad Nenndorf and at Camp 020, violence was taboo and that physical coercion was forbidden under his command.

After the war Latchmere House became a prison until it was closed in 2011. The site has now been redeveloped for housing.

Huntercombe House, near Henley-on-Thames, Oxfordshire

HMP Huntercombe is now a Category C men's prison near Henley-on-Thames but it started life as an internment camp during the Second World War. Also on the site was Camp 020R which acted as a reserve camp for Latchmere House. It housed longer-term detainees and is believed to have been one of the locations where the German Deputy Führer Rudolf Hess was held and questioned after his mysterious flight to Scotland in 1941.

Rudolf Hess

Mytchett Place in Surrey, not far from the military town of Aldershot across the border in Hampshire, had a unique role in the Second World War. Known under the code name of Camp Z, it had just one prisoner – Rudolf Hess. After initial questioning elsewhere, he spent over a year at the requisitioned manor house in conditions of high security.

He was interrogated at length, but it appears that the interviews yielded little useful information. Nor did the secret microphones bugging his rooms produce any vital intelligence useful to the Allied war effort. He behaved erratically and frequently claimed that his food was being poisoned.

Hess, who made a suicide attempt by throwing himself off a balcony, was deemed to be mentally ill and of no great strategic value to British intelligence. There are unconfirmed reports that exiled Polish officers tried to break into Mytchett Place to kidnap Hess in revenge for Nazi atrocities in Poland. A gun battle is said to have resulted.

Mytchett Place now houses the offices of a research company.

Rudolf Hess, the German Deputy Führer, was held at Mytchett Place in Surrey and later at Maindiff Court Hospital in South Wales after his mysterious solo flight from Germany in 1940. He was later sentenced to life imprisonment at the Nuremberg War Crimes Trials. (Bundesarchiv)

Mytchett Place in Surrey is now the headquarters of a research company but was Camp Z during the war with just one prisoner, Rudolf Hess. (Kamkorp)

Maindiff Court Hospital, Abergavenny, Wales

For the rest of the war from June 1942, Hess was confined to a hospital in South Wales. Most of Maindiff Court Hospital at Abergavenny was used for treating military casualties. Hess had his own room which was guarded. However, he was allowed a measure of freedom and was taken for trips out of the hospital in Abergavenny and the neighbouring countryside. No attempt was made to conceal the fact that Hess was in the hospital and there were reports in the national papers about his stay there. Local legend has it that he was known as the 'Kaiser of Abergavenny'. Hess left Maindiff Court at the end of the war and was taken to Nuremberg where he appeared at the War Crimes Trials. Hess escaped execution but was sentenced to life imprisonment. He served his sentence in Spandau Prison in Berlin where he hanged himself at the age of ninety-three in 1987.

Maindiff Court is still in use as a hospital.

Trent Park, near Cockfosters, London

Trent Park was an important centre for the interrogation of German officers and Luftwaffe pilots. It operated from the beginning of the war, using hidden microphones to listen in to their unguarded conversations, as well as traditional interrogation methods. Later in the war it was the location of the so-called Cockfosters Cage where a total of eighty-four captured German generals and several hundred lower-ranking officers were sent. They were treated well, given whisky and allowed walks in the grounds. Trent Park has been described as having almost had the atmosphere of a gentlemen's club. British intelligence believed that treating German generals, many of whom were not ardent Nazis, in this way was the most effective method of getting useful information. Intelligence about Germany's V1 and V2 rocket campaigns was among the most valuable information believed to have been gleaned at Trent Park.

Trent Park's grounds are now a country park and the house and other buildings, which formed a campus of Middlesex University until 2012, are now being redeveloped for housing. There is an active campaign underway to establish a museum at Trent Park to tell the story of the Second World War 'secret listeners'.

Wilton Park, Beaconsfield and Latimer House, Latimer, Buckinghamshire

Both these stately homes in Buckinghamshire were also used for the interrogation of high-ranking officers including U-boat captains and Luftwaffe pilots. Both employed the same bugging devices as at Trent Park and elsewhere. Immediately after the war, Wilton Park became a re-education centre for Germans and 4,500 people, mainly prisoners of war, were made to go there to be re-educated about democracy and western values. Later Wilton Park had a variety of military uses until 2014. As of 2018, plans had been drawn up to redevelop the site, including for housing. Latimer House is now a conference centre.

Farm Hall, Godmanchester, Cambridgeshire

This listed Georgian house not far from Huntingdon was at the heart of one of the most important intelligence gathering operations as the war ended. As the British and Americans advanced through Germany in the early months

A group of prominent German officers detained at Trent Park, near Cockfosters, north London in November 1944, including Heinrich Eberbach, the last General of the Panzertroope, second left in the front row. (Bundesarchiv)

of 1945, they were determined to capture as many as possible of the scientists involved in Germany's atomic bomb programme. This was to try to ensure that Germany was not in a position to deploy an atomic bomb, but also to try to keep the German nuclear knowledge away from the Russians.

Ten captured German scientists were taken to Farm Hall in Godmanchester and kept there for six months from the summer of 1945. Codenamed Operation Epsilon, it involved bugging their conversations to discover what they knew about the bomb and how close Germany had been to deploying one. The recordings were made public in 1993 but proved inconclusive. There have been claims that Germany's leading nuclear scientists deliberately tried not to succeed in making a bomb because they did not want to aid a Nazi victory. Others believe that Germany simply didn't have the necessary expertise or resources to achieve an atomic bomb.

Farm Hall, at Godmanchester in Cambridgeshire, where ten of Germany's leading scientists were held for six months from the summer of 1945 in Operation Epsilon to try to extract information from them about Germany's atomic weapons programme. (US National Archives)

Many of the scientists involved in the German atomic bomb programme went on to work for both the American and Soviet nuclear and space programmes after the war. Farm Hall is now a private residence.

Prisoner of War Camps

The special interrogation camps already discussed were of course only a very small fraction of the total number of prisoner of war camps in Britain by the end of the Second World War. An estimated 500,000 prisoners were accommodated in Britain by the end of the war and beyond, of whom about 400,000 were German and most of the rest, Italian.

After their initial screening at the various 'cages' and transit camps, most of the prisoners were not considered serious security risks. PoWs were placed in one of four categories: A 'white' were those considered to be positively anti-Nazi; B 'grey' were those considered to be less clearly anti-Nazi but still essentially unsympathetic to the Nazi regime; but C and C+ 'black' were considered to be either pro-Nazi or ardent Nazis. Category 'black' prisoners were sent to special camps, but the rest went to standard camps all over the country. The camps were located in a motley collection of locations including requisitioned country houses, unfinished council estates, former military barracks and many other places.

The timeline of the prisoner of war camp story is interesting. It was really only as the war turned decisively in the Allies' favour in 1943 and beyond that the numbers of PoWs reaching Britain's shores increased dramatically. The increase then stepped up markedly after D-Day in June 1944. Many of the temporary barracks set up in the early part of 1944 to house the millions of Allied service personnel waiting for the Normandy landings were subsequently pressed into service to house PoWs after D-Day.

It is also important to remember that large numbers of PoWs stayed in Britain for some time after the war ended in 1945. This was partly because of the logistics of repatriation but also because PoWs had become an important part of the workforce which Britain needed to retain to help counter the privations of post-war austerity. In addition, a significant number of PoWs wanted to stay and forge a new life in Britain, a country for which they had developed an affection during their captivity.

Overall, relationships between PoWs and the host population seem to have been harmonious. Most prisoners worked in the local community. Even though fraternisation with PoWs was forbidden under wartime regulations, relationships did develop. There is some evidence that PoWs, particularly Italians, were often viewed with sympathy by the local communities.

There were isolated incidents of tensions between local people and PoWs. For example, an Italian PoW was stabbed during a disturbance in Kew in London. The cause of the fracas appears to have been local anger at the Italian PoWs mixing with British women. On the other hand, an Italian doctor, held as a PoW in Cambridgeshire, saved a six-year-old boy from drowning in the River Cam and was given an award by the Royal Humane Society.

A final thought about PoW camps – in a way they disappeared almost as quickly as they had sprung up in the emergency of war. English Heritage has attempted to identify the location of the estimated 1,500 camps around

Harperley prisoner of war camp, near Crook in County Durham, is one of very few British PoW camps still standing in almost its original form in the twenty-first century. (Rolyat29)

Britain. By the early twenty-first century, all traces had pretty much vanished of many of them. There are thought to be only five camps still in existence and preserved in some way.

These are some examples of PoW camps around Britain:

Harperley near Crook, County Durham remains one of very few British PoW camps from the war which remains much as it was in the 1940s. More than forty huts are still standing in various states of repair. The camp, which was a standard one for low risk prisoners, could house up to 1,500 inmates. Italians were the first prisoners, but they were later replaced by Germans. The facilities on the site included a theatre built by the inmates. Harperley Camp had an orchestra which was very popular in the local community. Two local people bought the site in the 1990s and it was opened to the public as

From 2002 to 2005, Harperley Camp was opened to the public as a tourist attraction, but as of 2018 it remains closed and one of the huts is used by a local cheese-making company. (Alan Murray)

a tourist attraction from 2002 to 2005. As of 2018, one of the buildings at Harperley Camp was being used by a cheese making business.

Island Farm, Bridgend, South Wales achieved a certain celebrity status because it was the scene of the biggest escape from any British PoW camp during the war. On 11 March 1945 at least seventy German PoWs escaped from the camp after a long period of planning and digging tunnels. Most escapees were recaptured in the local area, but some reached as far as Birmingham and Southampton. It has been claimed that some evaded capture and found their way back to Germany. At the time of the escape, Island Farm housed German officers. Previously it had accommodated German and Italian PoWs. Earlier, it was a D-Day holding barracks for American troops and it had originally been built as a hostel for workers at the nearby munitions factory. One of the huts from the PoW camp is preserved on the site. In 2017, an archaeological study uncovered one of the escape tunnels still in good condition.

Cultybraggan Camp, Comrie, Perthshire, Scotland was a Black Camp for those PoWs classified as the most committed to Nazi ideals. It opened in 1941 and housed up to 4,000 prisoners. It was the scene of one of the most gruesome events in any British PoW camp. In 1944, the ringleaders of an escape plot centred on the American run camp at Devizes in Wiltshire were sent there. Also sent by mistake was Feldwebel Wolfgang Rosterg, an opponent of the Nazis. He was lynched by other inmates. Five PoWs were convicted of his murder and executed. After the war, the camp became a military training area and later a Cold War Regional Seat of Government bunker was built on the site.

Featherstone Camp, Haltwhistle, Northumberland was a large camp of huts originally opened to accommodate US forces prior to D-Day but it became, like Cultybraggan, a Black Camp for hardened Nazis. It was in operation until 1948 and was one of the largest camps in Britain with 200 huts and 4,000 officers. They came from all branches of the German military and were subject to a process of denazification during their stay at the camp. They attended lectures from university academics and others to try to inculcate democratic values to help the rebuilding of post-war Germany.

Eden Camp, Malton, North Yorkshire is now a Second World War Museum opened in 1987. Its wartime story is typical of many British camps. Originally opened as a camp for Italian PoWs in the middle of 1943, they were moved out late in 1943 when the camp became the base for Polish forces assembling for the D-Day landings. Late in 1944, the camp reverted to being a PoW camp housing captured Germans and it continued in this role until 1949.

Wollaton Hall Park Camp, Nottingham was a massive temporary camp set up to accommodate US troops in the build-up to D-Day. More than 2,000 paratroopers of the US 82nd Airborne Division were stationed there from March 1944. In Christmas of that year a PoW camp was established in the Park, built by Italians but eventually housing around 2,000 German PoWs. Many stayed for two years and local people recall the appeal that went

Eden Camp near Malton in North Yorkshire has been preserved and has been open as a Second World War Museum since 1987. During the war, it housed Italian and later German PoWs. (Eden Camp)

out towards the end of their stay for Nottingham families to invite PoWs into their homes for Christmas lunch, which many did.

Internment Camps

As well as incarcerating captured service personnel of enemy countries, all countries also locked up without trial the civilians of those countries living in their midst. They also often imprisoned their own citizens deemed to be a threat to national security. Internment has been a feature of war, and sometimes of peace, for many years and Britain in the Second World War was no exception.

The threat of invasion in 1940 produced a wave of anxiety, some might say hysteria, about 'the enemy within' and the dangers of a 'Fifth Column'. However, the internment of enemy aliens had begun as soon as the war started. On 1 September 1939, 415 suspected Nazi sympathisers, on a list compiled by the security service MI5, were rounded up and taken initially to Olympia in west London and later to a requisitioned holiday camp at Clacton-on-Sea in Essex.

A process of categorising the 73,355 Germans and Austrians living in Britain, many of whom were Jews who had fled from the Nazis, was also started. Those categorised as Class A were considered likely to help the Nazi war effort and were therefore a threat; Class B were considered a possible risk; and Class C were thought not to be problematical. A series of tribunals were held from the start of October 1939, conducted in secret, to determine the categorisation. A very small proportion were considered high-risk and placed in Category A – only 569; 6,782 were classed as 'B' but the overwhelming majority, 64,000 were 'C'. Of these 64,000, around 55,000 were deemed to be refugees from Nazi oppression.

However, in May 1940, as German forces advanced through the Low Countries and France, the atmosphere changed. After the Dunkirk evacuation and the start of the Battle of Britain, the threat of invasion was very real and this hostility to Germans and subsequently Italians was perhaps understandable. Internment of various categories of lower risk Germans and Austrians was progressively introduced. The tabloid newspapers were fuelling the flames with headlines like 'Intern the Lot'. When Italy entered the war in June 1940, Italian shops and businesses were attacked in various British cities; 4,000 Italians living in Britain were interned.

A total of around 30,000 Germans and Italians had been interned by the summer of 1940 and they were accommodated in a series of places in and beyond Britain. As with PoWs, the original intention had been to ship them overseas, principally to Canada. Several thousand internees, along with some early PoWs, were deported to Canada and to Australia. However, the policy was reined back after one ship, the SS *Arandora Star*, which set sail from Liverpool bound for Canada in July 1940, was sunk by a German U-boat with the loss of over 800 lives, including many people known to be opponents of the Fascist regimes in Italy and Germany.

The places used to house internees were fairly rudimentary. No real planning had gone into how and where to accommodate the many thousands of people scooped up by the new regulations imposed in the summer of 1940. Those who experienced incarceration in the many camps speak of poor conditions, bad food and a very hostile attitude to them from guards and soldiers.

Ettore Emanuelli, an Italian internee, was arrested under Defence Regulation 18b on 10 June 1940 and held in a number of the camps. He told the BBC in 2004 of his experiences at a number of internment camps:

A half-built council estate in Huyton in Merseyside was requisitioned and used as an internment camp. After the war, the estate was completed as the Woolfall Estate. (Unknown)

Walton Prison, Liverpool. An abandoned wing of the prison was reopened as an internment camp. Conditions were grim. The rooms were filthy with pigeon droppings everywhere. Food was basic. 'To this day', Ettore recalled, 'I have a dislike of porridge as it was served to us in battered aluminium basins.' Ettore spent seven weeks at Walton.

Bertram Mills Circus Winter Quarters, Ascot, Surrey was pressed into service as an internment camp, a sign of the desperate measures needed to deal with the problem. Even the elephant houses were used as accommodation. When Ettore arrived there from Liverpool, no arrangements had been made to feed the internees. Many of them had catering skills and they ended up largely organising their own cooking.

York Racecourse, York, North Yorkshire was Ettore's next port of call after nearly four months at the Circus in Ascot. At York, the main grandstand and administration buildings had been converted into a detention camp, surrounded by barbed wire and patrolled by guards. He spent sixteen weeks there.

Woolfall Estate, Huyton, Merseyside was one of the most curious of Second World War camps in Britain. It was a half-built council estate which was requisitioned and used as a camp. Ettore remembers living amidst builders' rubble. He recalled, 'I can remember supplementing our greens by using the dandelion leaves which grew in abundance around the site. The camp was surrounded by anti-aircraft guns which made it very difficult to sleep at night'. After the camp was closed at the end of the war, the estate was finished.

Camp 'M', Peel, Isle of Man was, like many internees, Ettore's final destination. There were ten internment camps on the island and a total of 14,000 internees were held there at its peak. Camp 'M' was in fact a row of terraced houses in Peel. Conditions there were much more favourable than Ettore's earlier camps with decent rations and internees doing their own cooking. Ettore was held there for just over a year from May 1941 until his eventual release in August 1942. Like many internees, he appeared before a tribunal and was deemed no longer to be a risk. Although male prisoners were still guarded, the regime for many internees on the Isle of Man was much more relaxed. They were allowed to work and to go on walks.

Kempton Park and Lingfield Racecourses were among the transit camps used to house internees for an initial period, as well as their role as 'cages' for PoWs. Another important internment camp was at **Warth Mills, Bury, Greater Manchester**. This disused cotton mill was hastily turned into an internment camp in 1940. The first arrivals, mainly Italian internees, had to clear the oily cotton waste from the floors. They were given very thin mattresses and had to sleep on the floor. There were only twenty toilets for the 2,000 inhabitants of the camp.

'Careless Talk' Defence Regulations

Measures designed to deal with the perceived threat of 'enemy aliens' on British soil during the Second World War were accompanied by extensive attempts to try to maintain morale, ensure a sense of secrecy and prevent dangerous behaviour by the indigenous population. It is often said that crime went up during the war, as indeed it did. However, much of that was because the number of crimes on the statute book went up dramatically to deal with the exigencies of war.

The legislation and regulations which created a myriad of new ways of breaking the law in wartime Britain were conceived in the febrile atmosphere of the 'Phoney War' over the winter of 1939-40 and the subsequent threat of invasion the following summer. Two Emergency Powers (Defence) Acts were passed, the first in 1939 and a second in 1940 which essentially gave the Government sweeping powers to conduct war. These included the power to create offences by Order of Council which were enshrined in the various sets of Defence Regulations which came into effect as the war progressed.

Cabinet papers from the time reveal the level of paranoia even at the top of Government. The then Home Secretary, Sir John Anderson, sent a note to Cabinet colleagues on 5 June 1940 urging discretion when dining in restaurants. He warned them of the dangers of their conversations being overheard by Italian waiters. The Home Secretary also wrote to Winston Churchill expressing concerns about the Foreign Secretary Lord Halifax living in the Dorchester Hotel and the security of government red boxes delivered to him there.

The belief in the danger of the 'enemy within' and a 'Fifth Column' led, among other things, to the creation of a range of new offences. The official record of crime in wartime Britain 'Criminal Statistics England and Wales, 1939 to 1945', published by the Home Office in 1947, lists thirty-six different categories of defence regulation offences including those related to misleading acts, interference with HM Forces, sabotage, photography, protected places and areas, looting and the publication of disturbing reports. There were also a range of offences related to matters like the blackout, use of public shelters, use of fuel, control of employment and industry. There were even offences related to the use of pigeons!

There were prosecutions and convictions for these new offences throughout the war. On 22 November 1942 the *Sunday Pictorial* reported that Peter Singleton, a 28-year-old Royal Army Service Corps driver, was sent to prison for two years after absconding from duty. He was apparently fed up with not being given the chance to fight in a front-line capacity. He vented his frustration during a visit to a canteen in Darlington when he was overheard saying that 'Britain will never drive Rommel out of Africa' and that 'British equipment was inferior and British officers lousy'. His two-year sentence was ordered for being absent without leave but also for 'creating despondency'.

In March 1942 a woman who spoke to an Army officer in a café in Hove expressed admiration for Hitler and claimed that Roosevelt and Churchill had Jewish blood. She was fined £50 (about £2,000 at 2018 values) and given

Propaganda poster produced by the Ministry of Information – part of the campaign to get people to keep quiet and not let out any secrets which might help the enemy. (National Archives)

a month's hard labour after being found guilty of 'publicising matters likely to cause alarm and despondency'.

On 21 May 1943 the *Liverpool Post* reported the story of 52-year-old Edward Ryan from Huyton under the headline 'Dangerous Talk – Penalty for a "Cock and Bull" Story'. Ryan had been heard while on fire-watching duty making various statements about the war, including claiming that thirty-five to forty ships had been lost in each of the last five convoys crossing the Atlantic. He claimed to have got this information from a friend whose son-in-law worked in the British Embassy in Madrid. Police investigations concluded that the information was false and that Ryan had made it up. The stipendiary magistrate hearing the case described Ryan's claims as 'just a cock-and-bull story – absolute nonsense', but nevertheless sent him to prison for a month with hard labour.

Other prosecutions for these specially created wartime offences included a ship's engineer fined £10 (around £400 in 2018) for taking pictures of a war ship in Liverpool; an Army major fined in November 1941 for defeatist talk in a London pub and a worker in a Rochester naval base in Kent, overheard in a pub discussing details of production in the base, being given a two-month sentence.

Alongside the legal sanctions, the British Government, mainly through the Ministry of Information, conducted a wide range of propaganda campaigns. Some were designed to boost morale, others to provide practical information (for example, about making the most of food rations) but others were aimed at warning people of the dangers of giving away information which could be useful to the enemy.

A Cabinet discussion in November 1939 led to the first of a number of major campaigns about the need for secrecy. A variety of methods were used to persuade the public of the need to avoid giving away important wartime information. These included the distribution of around 700,000 posters to hotels and public houses, munitions and other factories, Post Offices, local authority offices, railways and docks buildings and other locations. A special propaganda film was made, the newspapers printed articles, the BBC ran talks and there were reminders in every telephone kiosk about the need for secrecy. Many of the slogans used in these propaganda posters still resonate through the language three-quarters of a century later including 'Careless Talk Costs Lives', 'Keep Mum, She's Not So Dumb', and later 'Loose Lips Sink Ships' and 'Keep it under Your Hat.'

Throughout the war there were other campaigns emphasising the need for discretion and care in conversations. Many of these fuelled a sense of 'the enemy within' and also created a sense of suspicion and mistrust. Some resentment was expressed in wartime surveys of public opinion, but the anecdotal and statistical evidence suggests that the propaganda campaigns contributed to a very low level of indiscreet talk during the war.

Midway through the war, there was concern about whether punishments for 'Careless Talk' were severe enough. *The People* newspaper reported on 13 December 1942 that the Home Office had advised magistrates that they should impose stricter sentences for 'Careless Talk' offences. In 1943 the Home Office produced a paper proposing an increase in sentences under Defence Regulation 3. The proposal was to increase the maximum sentence to seven years' imprisonment. In the end, the penalties stayed the same, three months' imprisonment or £100 fine on summary conviction and two years' imprisonment or a £500 fine for conviction on indictment.

Politicians concluded that there were really two types of 'Careless Talk'. There were ordinary members of the public who, for a variety of motives, often vanity, wanted to pose as people in the know. They spread rumours and opinions, often untrue, in an attempt to impress friends and relatives. They could, where necessary, be dealt with under the various Defence Regulation offences.

More serious were people holding some sort of official position including workers in war production factories, at dockyards or on the railways. They did sometimes have access to important, and accurate, information and, if they started talking out of turn, the consequences were more likely to be serious. The Defence Regulations might not always be sufficient for these sorts of cases. However, another important weapon in the legal armoury was the Treachery Act, 1940. This had been added to the statute book at the height of fears of a German invasion amid concern that the existing offence of treason might be difficult to apply, particularly to German agents or spies. The Treachery Act defined the offence thus: 'If, with intent to help the enemy, any person does, or attempts or conspires with any other person to do any act which is designed or likely to give assistance to the naval, military or air operations of the enemy, to impede such operations of His Majesty's forces, or to endanger life, he shall be guilty of felony and shall on conviction suffer death.'

Sixteen people were sentenced to death for treachery during the war. Mostly, they were not British subjects and a majority were Germans, Dutch and Belgians working for German intelligence. The numbers were relatively so low because Britain was very successful both at capturing German agents and then at 'turning' so many of them into double agents.

There were a few Britons found guilty under the Treachery Act. On 3 November 1942 Duncan Scott-Ford was hanged at Wandsworth Prison in London after being found guilty under the Treachery Act of passing information relating to British convoys to a German agent. Oswald Job, born in London of German parents, was hanged at Pentonville Prison in London on 16 March 1944 for working for German intelligence. George Armstrong's execution took place on 10 July 1941 at Wandsworth after being found guilty of helping German intelligence in the United States.

So, did this combination of coercion and persuasion work? The basic answer would appear to be yes. The official criminal statistics for the war period reveal how few people ended up in front of the courts for 'Careless Talk' offences. The types of cases mentioned earlier were comparatively rare. At first sight a total of 1,275,889 convictions under the Defence Regulations between 1939 and 1945 seems a huge number. However, the overwhelming majority of these were for what were essentially infractions of the rules about the wartime economy, for example 928,397 were for offences related to the Control of Lights and Sounds, essentially breaches of the blackout regulations. Another 113,799 cases concerned breaches of the control of industry regulations, 68,219 for control of motor vehicles and 34,662 for control of employment. Whilst these offences were important in terms of the conduct of the war, they were not matters which affected secrecy and information.

The number of convictions for offences under the Defence Regulations for matters related most directly to secrecy was comparatively few. These included 1,930 people found guilty of 'misleading acts'; nearly 16,000 people convicted of various offences related to protected places, trespassing and loitering; 793 offences related to the postal system; 509 for photography offences; 361 for sabotage; 131 for 'publication of disturbing reports' and just 38 for 'interference with HM Forces'. Given the five-and-a-half year length of the war and a population of almost 50million people, these totals are very small.

Overall, then it is reasonable to conclude that the vast majority of Britons did heed the propaganda messages and did abide by the wartime regulations and 'kept Mum' for the duration of the conflict.

Chapter Eight

Weapons Of Mass Destruction

Rhydymwyn and Britain's other chemical weapons sites;
'Tube Alloys' – Britain's early Atomic bomb research;
'Churchill's Toyshop' and other secret weapons research.

Rhydymwyn M.S Valley Factory, Flintshire, Wales

Rhydymwyn was chosen as the site for Britain's main chemical weapons storage in 1939. Under international law at the time, it was illegal to use chemical weapons but not to make and store them. (Colin Philpott)

'It was a big secret and I never told anyone', were Rose Parry's opening words to me when I spoke to her just before Christmas 2017 about her wartime experiences. At the age of 97, Rose still has a vivid memory of her work as an inspector at the remote factory in North Wales which was at the heart of one of the most secretive parts of Britain's Second World War endeavours. For many years, she did keep quiet about what she had done there but now speaks about it openly.

Yet again the story of secret wartime locations throws up a site of quite exceptional historical significance in the most ordinary and innocuous of places. Rhydymwyn is a small village in the Alyn Valley in Flintshire not far from the England-Wales border, with a population of about 500, yet it was there that Britain made and stored massive quantities of chemical weapons throughout the war.

When I met Rose at her home in the seaside resort of Prestatyn, about 20 miles from Rhydymwyn, she explained that her job was to inspect the completed bombs.

> 'I had to make sure there weren't any spills. We had to check the empty cases before they were filled to make sure they were empty and then we had to check them after they'd been filled to make sure there hadn't been any spills. We had to check them all and keep records of everything.'

Rose described the security and safety precautions involved in the job.

'I had to sign the Official Secrets Act when I started there in 1941. We had to have a pass and had to show it at the gate house each day. Then when we arrived for work, we had to go into this room and take all our clothes off and have a shower before we put on the special factory clothes. At the end of our shift, we had to take off the factory clothes and they were washed each day. We had to shower again before we put our own clothes on to go home.'

However, the most remarkable aspect of Rose's recollections was her claim about what she knew about the work at the time.

'I had no idea that the weapons I was checking were chemical weapons,' Rose told me when I spoke with her in 2017. She is clearly troubled by the idea that she played a part in the production of such deadly weapons. 'There's not a good thing to say about it now,' she told me and nodded in agreement when I asked whether she now regretted having had to work there during the war.

Rose Parry worked at Rhydymwyn from 1941 until 1944 as an inspector checking chemical weapons. (Rhydymwyn Valley History Society)

Although it is perhaps tempting to conclude that Rose is choosing to believe that she was ignorant of the true nature of the operation at the factory where she worked during the war, it could be true. As has been seen at other places, the principle of 'need to know' and of compartmentalisation of roles in wartime factories was a strong one. So, it is quite possible that Rose Parry spent three years of her life handling deadly weapons without realising the dangers she was facing. Rose handed in her notice in June 1944, by coincidence on D-Day. Earlier that year, she had lost a baby and had been in hospital for a while recovering.

The Rhydymwyn site had been identified in the spring of 1939 as a suitable location for a concealed manufacturing and storage site for chemical weapons. Britain had used chemical weapons of various sorts during the First World War. Between the wars it had been a signatory to the Geneva Protocol which banned the use of chemical and biological weapons, although not their development and manufacture. During the 1930s, Britain believed that Germany was making and stockpiling chemical weapons and that it needed to do the same. The first development of chemical weapons took place at other sites but many of these were potentially vulnerable to bombing. The search began for a bomb-proof and remote location.

In August 1939 the Treasury approved spending of £546,000 (about £32million at 2018 values) to start construction in the Alyn Valley; 1,000 people worked on the construction of what became known as MS Factory, Valley. It was a good location because of its plentiful water supply, its relative proximity to a supply of labour from Merseyside and its closeness to the established chemical industries of Cheshire and Lancashire. Above all, though, being in a wooded valley meant that it was largely concealed and therefore much less vulnerable to bombing.

Several cavernous buildings were put up at the site. They were used to make Runcol, a type of mustard gas; they were also used to fill munitions with gas made at other factories; and to convert substances made elsewhere to make them usable in weapons. In total 15,477 tons of Runcol were made at Rhydymwyn between 1941 and 1945. In addition, there were extensive tunnels where weapons produced at Rhydymwyn and elsewhere were stored. It is estimated that some 500 tons of mustard gas was stored there in 100 5-ton buried tanks.

Over 2,200 people worked at Valley at the peak of its operation. Most of the management were from ICI and came from other parts of the country and many of the workers came from Liverpool and surrounding areas. There were only a few local people employed there. There was careful segregation

Between 1941 and 1945 15,477 tons of Runcol were made at Rhydymwyn, and an estimated 5.2million munitions were produced in total. (Colin Philpott)

of senior staff who had full knowledge of the operation and other groups of staff who may not have done. However, everyone working there had to sign the Official Secrets Act and it seems the nature of what was happening at the factory was not known. Mike Gibson from Prestatyn told the BBC in 2010 that he had lived as a boy at a local hotel run by his father near the factory. Several workers from the factory stayed at the hotel.

> 'However, they were not your average run of the mill workers; these men were from London and were obviously from the Ministry. They used to wear the traditional long black overcoats and trilbies, and would come home from work, have their evening meal, have a few pints in the bar and then to bed. They never revealed just what they did on the site – well, so my dad used to say.'

A decoy site to confuse potential enemy bombers was established about three miles away from the factory in 1941. The Luftwaffe's bombers reached north Wales on many occasions but the Rhydymwyn site was never hit.

It is, of course, the case that chemical weapons were used in the Second World War. Germany used them in a most horrific way in the gas chambers of the concentration camps, killing six million Jews and other people. Neither the Allies nor the Axis powers are thought to have used them in the general conduct of the war. So, the vast quantities of chemical weapons made and stored at Rhydymwyn were never used.

However, there is evidence that Britain would have been prepared to use them. Chemical weapons were taken to France by the British Expeditionary Force with a view to deploying them in retaliation had the Germans used them. These weapons had to be withdrawn at the time of the Dunkirk evacuation. Plans were drawn up to deploy chemical weapons on the beaches of south-east England in the event of a German invasion in 1940. It also appears that consideration was given to using them in bombing attacks on German cities in the latter stages of the war.

Several other sites, mostly in north-west England, were also involved in the research, manufacture and storage of Britain's chemical weapons. They were:

Sutton Oak, St Helen's, Merseyside. Sutton Oak had produced chemical weapons during the First World War. Between the wars it became the Chemical Defence Research Establishment and was involved in a variety of tests to determine the effect of exposure to chemical weapons. However, it also became a *de facto* manufacturing site as it had scale models of chemical

Many of the original buildings at Rhydymwyn, where over 2,000 worked during the war, still remain. They were cleared of their chemical weapons after the war and today the area is a nature reserve. (Colin Philpott)

weapons production plants in place already. For a short period in 1939-1940, when it was decided that Britain needed to increase its production dramatically, it was the sole manufacturer of chemical weapons while other sites, including Rhydymwyn, were still under construction. For most of the war and afterwards, Sutton Oak reverted to being a research base for the development of new chemical weapons, including Sarin. The plant was closed in the 1950s and an industrial estate now occupies the site.

Randle Works, Wigg Island, Runcorn, Cheshire. The small island between the River Mersey and the Manchester Ship Canal is now a country park. It was the location of the first new purpose-built chemical weapons plant started in 1937 and expanded rapidly in 1939. There were five buildings capable of producing over 300 tons of Runcol and Pyro gas a week. Randle

Everyone who worked at Rhydymwyn had to sign the Official Secrets Act. Managers from ICI were involved in the running of the plant and many of the workers there were brought in from other areas. (Colin Philpott)

Works had the capacity to store 500 tons of mustard gas in tunnels. After the war, the site was operated by ICI until the 1960s.

Springfields, Salwick, Preston, Lancashire. Springfields is now a nuclear site but, along with Randle and Rhydymwyn, it was one of three factories for manufacturing mustard gas.

There was also a phosgene factory at **Rocksavage, near Runcorn** and three factories were built to provide the constituents for the mustard gas factories at **Hillhouse, near Fleetwood in Lancashire**, at **Royd Mills near Huddersfield in West Yorkshire** and at **Wade in Cheshire**.

In addition, there were five Forward Filling Depots where mustard gas was stored near to airfields and army depots so that it could be brought into action

Sutton Oak at St Helen's, the HQ of the Chemical Defence Research Establishment, was involved in testing exposure to chemical weapons. For a short period in 1939-1940, it was the sole manufacturer of chemical weapons while other sites, including Rhydymwyn, were still under construction. (Sutton Beauty and Heritage)

quickly if needed. One of these, **Lord's Bridge, Barton, Cambridgeshire** to the west of Cambridge, became an ammunition dump at the beginning of the war but later in the war also housed a chemical weapons store. It was used for the bulk storage of mustard gas bombs close to bomber aircraft bases. It is now the site of the Mullard Radio Astronomy Observatory run by the University of Cambridge.

The other four Forward Filling Depots were: **Little Heath at Barnham Heath in Suffolk; Norton Disney, Lincolnshire; Melchbourne, Bedfordshire and Escrick in North Yorkshire**.

Two other important chemical weapons sites deserve a mention:

Porton Down, near Salisbury, Wiltshire has now become Britain's principal chemical weapons research and testing facility. It started life in the

Gruinard Island near Ullapool was the scene of a test by scientists from Porton Down of anthrax on sheep to determine whether it might be used in attacks on German cities, an idea which was abandoned. (Unknown)

First World War and by the time of the Second World War was a Chemical Defence Experimental Station, mainly concerned with tests on the possible use of biological weapons.

Gruinard Island, near Ullapool, Scottish Highlands was the scene of a biological weapons test by scientists from Porton Down in 1942. They wanted to test the impact of anthrax with a view to considering whether it could be used in attacks on German cities. Sheep were taken to the island and anthrax spores were exploded, killing the sheep within days of exposure. The conclusion of the tests was that use of anthrax on German cities would be deadly and far-reaching, leaving the cities uninhabitable for decades into the future. After the war, there was a long-running controversy about the decontamination of the island which was only finally declared safe by the Government in 1990.

Back at Rhydymwyn, its role in Britain's chemical weapons story continued long after the war. Most chemical weapon production in Britain stopped in 1945 but by that point there were considerable stockpiles. In addition, supplies of German chemical weapons, seized after the end of the conflict, were brought back to Britain. In June 1946, there were estimated to be 14,200 tons of mustard gas in Britain. In the following years much of that was assembled at Rhydymwyn and either destroyed there or buried at sea. It remained in use as a weapons store until the late 1950s.

Since then the site was retained by the Government as an emergency supplies store. Food supplies are said to have been stored there. There were plans to use it as a store for the Bank of England's gold and it was considered as an alternative to Corsham for the Government nuclear war bunker. However, neither of these plans materialised. In the 1990s and early 2000s, the site was decommissioned with some of its original buildings demolished and measures taken to reduce the risks from any toxic traces which might remain there. Nevertheless, Rhydymwyn remains on the international list of chemical weapons sites.

Today, many of the buildings and the tunnels remain and the area is managed as a nature reserve. The Rhydymwyn Valley History Society organises tours of the site. Walking inside the now empty shells of buildings where the deadly weapons were made is a chilling and evocative experience. At least there is some comfort in knowing that the products of this sinister location were never used.

'Tube Alloys' – The First Attempts at an Atomic Bomb

The Rhydymwyn story does not, however, end there. As well as its central role in the story of Britain's Second World War chemical weapons, it was also at the epicentre of the first attempts at creating a British atomic bomb, attempts which did eventually lead to a weapon that was, of course, used at the very end of the war.

In 2018 Eileen Doxford was believed to be the last surviving person who worked on the 'Tube Alloys' project', the codename for the British atomic bomb programme. When she joined the Wrens at the age of 19 she was given a choice of three jobs and rejected two of them but thought the third sounded interesting, even though she wasn't told much about it.

'I didn't want to go to the first two and the third one sounded more interesting. It was in north Wales. You would be doing this work which would help in peace time as well as war time. When I went down there this Doctor of Science interviewed me and said

Eileen Doxford worked on atomic weapons testing at Rhydymwyn. In 2018, she was the last known survivor of the team who worked on 'Tube Alloys', Britain's early attempts to create an atomic bomb. (Rhydymwyn Valley History Society)

that he couldn't tell me what we would be doing because only two people knew what we were actually doing and I'd got to accept that whatever it was, it was to be of as much help in peace time as it was in war time. He hoped that I would go and of course I duly did and I was billeted in Mold.'

Eileen spent three years working at the Valley works. The work on nuclear weaponry was centred on the P6 building there. It had been built originally for manufacturing Pyro chemical weapons but was never used for that purpose and was converted to be the secret test laboratory for early atomic weapons. Eileen recalled the secrecy which meant that she and her colleagues on Tube Alloys were largely segregated from the rest of the people working on the site.

'We were segregated, and we were very much made aware of it too. They felt we were sort of invading their territory. After I had to move from this billet in Mold and went up to this one in Buckley, there were already two girls there. They worked in the other part of the factory. Of course, they quizzed me like mad because they all wondered what we were doing. They said, "what is it that you're doing, why aren't you all open with the factory?" and I said "well, I'm sorry but I can't tell you what I'm doing". They were really 'hoitey-toitey' about it and I suppose they just had to accept it in the end, but it would have been easier if I could have told them but I couldn't and that was the end of it. I couldn't talk about it when I went home either.'

Eileen's job involved measuring and recording the experiments.

'I worked with this glass apparatus and I had a pump because I had to pump this apparatus down to below atmospheric pressure and I should also say that there was a little instrument attached to this which was called a 'pirani', which earned me the name of Pirani Queen. I had to calibrate what was happening. I would have a piece of graph paper and down one side I would put the pressures as it went down and I suppose along the bottom would be the time.'

The work at Rhydymwyn was the culmination of the deliberations of the MAUD Committee which was established in June 1940 to consider how

Britain could develop atomic weapons and whether it could do so before the Germans. Throughout the 1930s, since the discovery of nuclear fission, scientists in several countries including Britain had been working on the possibility of utilising this scientific knowledge to create deadly weapons. Research work was concentrated at four British universities – Birmingham, Liverpool, Oxford and Cambridge. In July 1941, two MAUD reports were produced which led to the creation of a joint British-Canadian project to try to create a bomb. Winston Churchill authorized the go-ahead for the project on 30 August 1941.

The expectation was that it would take two years and cost £50million (over £2billion at 2018 prices) to make a bomb. Oxford University's Clarendon Labs, Birmingham University, ICI at Billingham, Widnes and Runcorn,

As well as its role in the manufacture and storage of chemical weapons, Rhydymwyn was also the base for early work on developing an atomic bomb before Britain combined forces with the United States and Canada under the 'Manhattan Project'. (Colin Philpott)

Liverpool University, Metropolitan Vickers at Trafford Park, Manchester and the Cavendish Laboratory at Cambridge were all involved in the project.

The crucial process involved gaseous diffusion of uranium. Metropolitan Vickers were contracted to make four pilot gaseous units at their Trafford Park factory at a cost of £150,000 (£6million in 2018 prices). Three of these units were installed in building P6 at Rhydymwyn. ICI's Research Director, Wallace Akers, was chosen to run the project. The name 'Tube Alloys' was apparently chosen randomly to be completely meaningless and to be so vague as to give no indication of its true nature.

The work continued in the remote Welsh valley for more than two years. However, the United States was already pursuing its own nuclear weapons research. With superior resources at America's disposal, Britain and Canada eventually conceded that it was in the Allies' overall best interests to merge the projects, particularly given the fact that Germany was known also to be trying to make an A-Bomb. In addition, it made sense to site the gaseous diffusion process in America well away from the range of German air raids. On 19 August 1943 Britain, Canada and America signed the Quebec Agreement which effectively merged the Tube Alloys Project with the Americans' Manhattan Project and the three countries worked together for the remainder of the war. Thus, the Allies beat the Germans in the race for an atomic bomb. In August 1945, two bombs were dropped on the Japanese cities of Hiroshima and Nagasaki killing an estimated 130,000 people at the time and many more later through the effects of radiation. The devastation did, however, bring about Japan's surrender and the end of the Second World War.

After the war Anglo–American collaboration on nuclear matters came to an abrupt end and the post-war Labour Government, led by Clement Attlee, decided in 1947 that Britain would pursue the building of its own nuclear deterrent once more. On 3 October 1952, the first British nuclear device was successfully exploded in the Monte Bello islands off the coast of Australia. However, Rhydymwyn played no part in this as its nuclear weapons role finished at the end of the war and its test units were moved to new facilities at Didcot and Harwell in Oxfordshire.

Other Weapons Research

As well as chemical and atomic weapons, Britain invested much effort in the development of other special weapons. Among places where this work took place were:

Fort Halstead, near Sevenoaks, Kent was originally part of a nineteenth-century plan for a series of fortifications to protect the southern and eastern approaches to London. In 1938 it became the main centre of British military research into rockets and the base of the Projectile Development Establishment. Building F11 at Fort Halstead is listed by Historic England as a structure of historical importance because it is understood to be the earliest surviving building associated with British rocket research. It is believed that the site played a role in the wartime work on Britain's atomic bomb and it certainly did so after the war.

Fort Halstead retained a role in atomic weapons research until the 1950s and later became a more general government defence research establishment. The site has now been sold to developers who, as of 2018, are planning to build 450 homes and to create a new community there.

Now awaiting redevelopment for housing, Fort Halstead near Sevenoaks has been through various iterations as a highly secret defence establishment. In 1938 it became Britain's main centre for research into rockets, a key element in the development of the atomic bomb programme. (Kent Life)

Silvermere, Cobham, Surrey was the location for some of the early tests of the 'bouncing bomb' developed by Barnes Wallis and eventually used with destructive effect in the 'Dambuster' raids. Staff from Vickers at Weybridge had set up a base for the experimental work at nearby Foxwarren Park and they used the lake for their early tests. Barnes Wallis is said to have rowed out onto the lake in 1942 and fired different shaped models from a catapult to test his ideas. Later, the early mechanisms for releasing and spinning the bombs were tested there. The site is now a golf course with associated leisure facilities.

Clumber Park, near Worksop, Nottinghamshire is now a vast National Trust property not far from the A1. Once the home of the Dukes of Newcastle, the estate had fallen on hard times during the Depression of the 1930s and the house was demolished in 1938. The estate was taken over for military use at the beginning of the war. Among the things that happened there was the testing of the 'Nellie' tanks, a project which Winston Churchill had pushed forward as worthy of development at the start of the war. He believed that machines that could move forward, cutting a wide trench thus allowing infantry to advance more easily behind them, would be a useful addition to Britain's armoury. The project was codenamed Naval Land Equipment Tractors which was shortened to 'Nellie'.

Winston Churchill visiting Clumber Park in Nottinghamshire in August 1941 to witness trials of a new 'super-tank' known as 'Nellie' capable of digging a trench 2 metres wide and 1.5 metres deep for advancing troops. The trials were deemed only a limited success and the project was abandoned. (National Trust)

Five prototypes were built in Lincoln and Clumber Park was chosen for testing. Churchill himself witnessed one of the trials there in August 1941. 'Nellie' was 23 metres long, 2 metres wide, 2.5 metres high and made in two sections. The main section, driven on caterpillar tracks, looked like a greatly elongated tank and weighed 100 tons. The front section, weighing another 30 tons, was capable of digging a trench 1.5 metres deep and two metres wide. However, although the trials were deemed a limited success, the project was cancelled in 1943. By then the idea of a heavy, cumbersome machine, more suited to the static battlefronts of the First World War, was no longer relevant. 'Nellie' was consigned to history and the prototypes were dismantled.

'Churchill's Toyshop', The Firs, Whitchurch, Buckinghamshire

The final port of call on this journey is one of the most intriguing and wacky of all. It plays to the stereotype of British cunning and inventiveness. Known colloquially as 'Churchill's Toyshop', a country house in Buckinghamshire was the setting for developing a whole host of unconventional weapons. Some were eccentric flights of fancy, but others were deadly serious and were used in anger during the conflict.

The Firs, a mansion just off the High Street in the village of Whitchurch near Aylesbury in Buckinghamshire, was requisitioned to be the base for Department MD1 (Ministry of Defence 1). The department effectively reported directly to the Prime Minister who had set it up to try to cut through what he saw as bureaucratic inefficiencies in the weapons procurement process. Its base was originally in London but a country house in the countryside was regarded as a safer place for its secret research. The soubriquet, 'Churchill's Toyshop' was apparently given to The Firs by disgruntled Ministry of Defence officials whose processes were circumvented by the existence of the department.

Among the weapons invented at The Firs were: delay fuses, which could be timed to delay for up to a week before they set off; delayed jumping bombs which consisted of clusters of bombs which would explode at different times; limpet mines which were attached to their targets by magnets; the 'W Bomb', a delayed action underwater bomb for use against river traffic; aluminium strips, known as 'Window', dropped by planes which would confuse enemy radar; and the so-called Castrator cartridges which, sunk in the ground in a tube, would fire a bullet at a man's groin. Nearly all of these, and other inventions at The Firs were used extensively at various stages in the conflict.

An innocuous looking country house, The Firs, at Whitchurch near Aylesbury was the base for what became known as 'Churchill's Toyshop' – the base for Department MD1 which developed ingenious new weapons for use by the Special Operations Executive and others. (Coleshill Auxiliary Research Team)

After Churchill was voted out of office in 1945, the department was disbanded and its wartime story remained largely unknown until the 1970s when its former second-in-command, Stuart Macrae published a book, *Winston Churchill's Toyshop*. The Firs is now the base for various small businesses.

Conclusion

So, in conclusion, how are we to sum up the story of the many and varied locations, to a greater or lesser extent secret, that played a part in Britain's war effort between 1939 and 1945?

The single strongest impression left after studying hundreds of these places is the scale of the enterprise undertaken by Britain during those years. A country which reluctantly entered a conflict, which turned out to be the most costly and devastating in human history, marshalled its people and resources with a truly astonishing level of organisational ruthlessness. It is of course a matter of deep and terrible sadness that so many lives in so many countries had to be lost or ruined and that so many resources had to be wasted on war. However, given that the decision was taken to fight, it was done so with the full force of the state and of its economy thrown behind it.

By 1944, 55 per cent of Britain's national income was devoted to defence compared with just 6 per cent in 1938. Despite a cut of 50 per cent in imported raw materials during the war years, Britain achieved its highest ever recorded industrial output. The number of people employed in munitions rose from 1,150,000 in 1939 to 4,300,000 in 1944. Over the same period, the number of women working either in the services or munitions increased from 500,000 to 2,460,000. As the range and scope of conscription was extended as the war went on, the overwhelming majority of fit and healthy adults was engaged in the war effort in some way or other, whether young or old, male or female, by the end of the conflict.

The use of land and resources was planned, controlled and organised by the State which gave itself significant extra powers to requisition property, to control every aspect of the economy and to direct the lives of its citizens. This was a command economy of the first order. No space was wasted. Factories were turned over to wartime uses, country houses to secret wartime headquarters of one sort or another, farmers' fields became dummy and decoy airfields and cities. Where new buildings were needed, be they deep underground bunkers or vast concealed armaments factories, they

Thousands of factories across Britain, like the Rootes factory in Coventry, produced the armaments and machines needed for the war and the amount of bomb damage these factories suffered was relatively low. (Rootes Collection at the Coventry Archives and Research Centre)

were put up at great speed. Whole areas of the country effectively became no-go military areas in the run-up to D-Day.

All this was done almost without reference to the cost. Britain owed £3billion to overseas creditors and governments by 1945 which is the equivalent of £120billion at 2018 values. Britain's debt to the United States was only finally paid off in the early twenty-first century. Britain's total national debt at the end of the war was around £21billion (around £800billion at 2018 values) and it represented more than 200 per cent of the country's GDP. Many of us would wish that such impressive organisational ambition and deployment of resources might be used for beneficial purposes in peacetime.

What's more, when Britain faced a real and present danger, necessity was indeed the mother of invention. The lengths to which Britain went in its inventiveness to try to give itself and its Allies a critical advantage can only be described as impressive. The codebreaking operation centred on Bletchley Park, the painstaking work on decoys and dummies and the use of cutting edge science and technology to develop new deadly weapons, were all examples of phenomena that gave Britain and its Allies marginal but decisive advantages. In the darkest days of 1940 and 1941, faced with the threat of invasion, Britain still considered that the investment of time and resources in some of these ideas was worthwhile, even though they might have seemed fanciful at the time.

Of course, not everything went smoothly. Some aspects of the wartime economy were planned some time before war became inevitable, for example the building of shadow factories. However, other things were rather cobbled together at the last minute like the dummy and decoy programme. And, even though this was a war to preserve democratic values, many of those self-same values were sacrificed for the duration of the war as the ends were deemed to justify the means. At one end of the spectrum, there was the routine wartime control of everyday life, including rationing, censorship and blackouts. At the more sinister end were internment and methods of interrogation of enemy agents which arguably broke international law and contradicted the very values Britain was fighting to maintain.

But what of the secrecy of the locations featured in this book? There is a tendency, encouraged by war-based fiction and the tabloid end of television history programmes, to portray the war as having been conducted from a series of secret underground citadels. The claim is that these places remained completely hidden from view throughout the war because of the strictness of security, the cleverness of concealment and the loyalty of citizens. The word 'bunker' has a lot to answer for. The reality is rather more nuanced and there were several different types of location, all critical to the war effort, which operated with different levels of secrecy.

Command and control centres, the places from which the war was directed, were generally the best protected and many were indeed bunkers buried beneath ground, including the Cabinet War Rooms, the Battle of Britain bunker at Uxbridge and the bunkers buried in the cliffs of Dover from where the Dunkirk evacuation was masterminded. These were generally staffed by service personnel subject to military discipline as well as the most senior politicians and they were heavily guarded.

The country's industrial powerhouses were simply too numerous and required too much space to be buried beneath ground. Britain simply did its best to protect these above ground as best it could, through a mixture of camouflage, guards and decoy and dummy sites to confuse bombers. This was remarkably successful with only around a quarter of the country's key installations bombed and the lasting damage caused by those attacks relatively modest.

A great deal of Britain's war infrastructure was 'hidden in plain sight'. So, for example, the codebreaking centre at Bletchley Park was guarded by military police and its staff were rigorously checked and exhorted to keep quiet about what they did. But they worked through the war in a country house only partially concealed by surrounding woodland. It was almost as though it was hidden by not drawing too much attention to it. This was true of countless other wartime locations up and down the country.

The former wartime Avro aircraft factory near Leeds–Bradford Airport is now a distribution centre for many household consumer brands. (Colin Philpott)

And a crucial factor that contributed to the overwhelmingly successful protection of so many of the wartime locations was the principle of dispersal and duplication. A great deal of effort was put into making sure that too many eggs were not put in one basket. Hence, the five out-stations for Bletchley Park, the principle of shadow factories to which production could be switched if another was taken out of commission, the BBC's reserve studios away from its main London base and the provision of an almost replica copy of the Cabinet War Rooms buried under an ordinary suburban street in north-west London. In reality, much of this reserve capacity was never needed.

However, there is little doubt that ordinary Britons did by and large play their part in protecting the secrecy of key wartime installations and important wartime information. An assessment of the true state of wartime morale in Second World War Britain is beyond the ambit of this book. However, the overwhelming sense gleaned from conversations with those who lived through it, is that the vast majority of British people accepted, albeit reluctantly, the need for the war and endured it with a grim, stoical determination.

The image of the 'People's War' with a nation united behind its leaders to defeat Hitler and the evils of Nazism and defiant even in the horrors of the Blitz is too simplistic. Equally, there is a danger in giving too much emphasis to examples of bad behaviour on the home front including looting, fiddling rationing books, forging doctor's certificates to avoid call-up, black marketeering and other misdemeanours. All these and more undoubtedly existed but, as Robert Mackay concludes in his study of wartime Britain, 'Morale and belief in the need for war survived even the 1940 blitz and the real fear of invasion.'

This commitment to the cause undoubtedly manifested itself in a general heeding of the famous message that 'Careless Talk Costs Lives'. As we have seen, the number of prosecutions for breaches of the group of wartime offences related to giving away information important to the war effort was very small. For example, fewer than 2,000 people were convicted for 'misleading acts' and only 131 for the 'publication of disturbing reports'. The number of people found guilty of treason or treachery was miniscule.

There are a number of factors which clearly contributed to this. Britain was a much more deferential society than it is in the twenty-first century and people were far more likely to accept what they were told by those in authority. It was much more difficult to spread information than it is now. There was no Facebook or Twitter! The propaganda messages of the 'Careless

Talk' and other campaigns did seem to resonate with people particularly because they created a sense that people did not want to do anything which might endanger 'the boys on the front line'. The fear of prosecution and the shame of appearing in court and even being sent to prison for 'blabbing' were a deterrent.

In addition, even those engaged in more secret activities were often unaware of the full story about the activities with which they were involved. Many of the country's most sensitive operations were cleverly compartmentalised and operated on a strictly 'need to know' basis. Many of the locations where they took place were quite remote. And, even if local people were aware of what was happening on their doorstep, some undoubtedly kept quiet partly because they recognised the economic value of the activity which had fortuitously arrived in their neighbourhood. This was certainly true at places like the radar research station at Worth Matravers in Dorset.

Intelligence work conducted in great secrecy during the war is now commemorated on the Codebreakers Wall in the grounds of Bletchley Park. (Colin Philpott)

Above all, it is perhaps not surprising that people by and large kept their mouths shut because they knew Britain was engaged in a struggle which was truly existential in nature. This was not a distant war in a far-flung place but a fight for survival and the British way of life.

In her study of wartime Britain, Juliet Gardiner concludes that the story of the Second World War in Britain is one of 'courage and cowardice, of selflessness and opportunism, of great vision and intense scepticism, of stoic endurance and great anger…. Ultimately it remains a story of a sort of patriotism that was mostly not triumphalist or flag-waving, and even managed to ally itself to a dilute form of socialism.'

Again, it's beyond the scope of this book, but the spirit of wartime Britain undoubtedly forged a new social reality which manifested itself in post-war Britain. Women were empowered by their involvement in the war. Many people, men and women, gained new experiences of taking responsibility. The country became more equal with rationing and other measures offering a vision for many of a fairer society. Winston Churchill may have been a great wartime leader and an example of 'Cometh the hour, cometh the man' but the pre-war imperial values he represented were rejected by voters at the end of the war as Clement Attlee's Labour Party swept to power.

There are two additional points which form important codicils to the story of Britain's wartime secret locations, both of which offer important correctives to the traditional narrative of the war. Firstly, the most prevalent images of the Home Front of 1939 to 1945 are often centred on London and the south-east. From newsreels, one might form the impression that the Blitz was something inflicted only on the capital. Of course, London and the south-east of England suffered very much during the war, but so did many other parts of Britain. The spread of locations featured in this book demonstrates that, for a variety of reasons, much of the country's wartime infrastructure was deliberately located away from the most vulnerable part of the country. Every region of Britain was affected and contributed.

Secondly, many of the locations featured in this book were staffed very significantly by women. Munitions factories were overwhelmingly female, which put Britain's women very much in the front-line of exposure to danger. Even in the more rarefied atmosphere of the control bunkers of the Cabinet War Room, RAF Command HQs and elsewhere, Wrens and others were crucial members of the team. So, these two factors form a necessary counterbalance to the traditional concentration on the plucky Eastenders and heroic RAF pilots, important though they were.

So finally, what of the places themselves, secret to a greater or lesser extent during the war? One of the most remarkable aspects of this story is that so many of them remained secret for many, many years after the war had long since ended. The secrets of Bletchley Park, of Rhydymwyn, of The Paddock at Dollis Hill and many other places were kept for at least a generation and sometimes much longer. There are two main reasons for this. Firstly, the natural tendency of the British establishment towards secrecy and lack of openness clearly contributed. Secondly, however, there were powerful political reasons why the British authorities wanted to keep a lid on activities that had helped win the war. For example, the code-breaking that had helped defeat Germany was immediately directed against the new enemy, and former ally, the Soviet Union. Likewise, the secrets of nuclear weaponry were important in the emerging Cold War between the West and the Russians. Many of the physical locations were themselves useful in this regard as well.

However, the people who had taken a vow of secrecy during the war also kept silent in many cases for years afterwards. Even today, some who signed the Official Secrets Act clearly feel somewhat perturbed that the work they did in conditions of secrecy three quarters of a century ago is now openly discussed. For some, it was simply a matter of honour. They had signed the Act and they took it seriously, but there was also an element of wanting to get on with their lives.

With the benefit of hindsight, we can now look back at the period to 1945 with the rose-coloured tint of a successful outcome of the war. The work of codebreakers and others is rightly lauded as a key part of the story of the defeat of Nazism. However, the reality for those involved back in 1945 was that they had lived through six-and-a-half years of war and they were glad to see the back of it. Most people didn't talk about the war, some because they had witnessed horrors they would rather forget, but others because they were glad to be rid of work that seems heroic now, but was hard and repetitive then.

Britain's secret wartime locations have themselves enjoyed a variety of fates. Some of course have been recognised, often only recently, for their historical significance and have been memorialised and made into museums and visitor attractions, like Bletchley, the Churchill War Rooms and the Western Approaches Command in Liverpool. Others have reverted to their pre-war use, including many of the country houses, sports stadia and other locations requisitioned in 1939. Some gained new uses in the post-war world, often associated with the Cold War, like the underground bunker at

Although described by Winston Churchill as 'a piece of useless folly', The Paddock alternative cabinet war rooms were an example of the lengths to which Britain's planning went to provide back-up locations for vital wartime facilities. (Colin Philpott)

Kenton in Newcastle or the shadow factories built for war which were put to peaceful use, making cars or tractors or other products. Many though have disappeared altogether. The radar stations that dotted the wartime coastline, the decoy and dummy airfields, the hideouts of the British Resistance have to all intents and purposes vanished.

A very few have been frozen in aspic, left pretty much as they were in 1945, not memorialised but also not converted for other uses. It is perhaps these places, like the abandoned chemical factory in north Wales and the alternative war rooms in north London which, for me at least, are the most poignant traces of secret wartime Britain. Official secrecy can, of course, be a convenient cover for political obfuscation, chicanery and all manner of abuse of state power. In twenty-first century Britain, it is not, in my

Entrance to the tunnels at Rhydymwyn MS Valley Works in North Wales where Britain's vast Second World War chemical weapons store was kept but never used. (Colin Philpott)

view, to be generally encouraged. Nevertheless, at a time of existential threat between 1939 and 1945, it was clearly important. The silent relics of Rhydymwyn and of The Paddock and many other places are testament to the vital role played by the ordinary people of Britain in keeping quiet in the Second World War.

Sources

Original Sources

National Archives Documents: PREM 4/37/9A, HO 144/21975, HO 201/30, HO 201/27, HO 201/28, HO 201/42, HO 201/20, HO 201/23, HO 201/22, HO 201/19, HO 201/36, HO 45/19510, CAB 67/2/38.

City of Coventry Archives at the Coventry Archives and Research Centre: CCA/3/1 7600, 7601, 7603, 7604, 7606, 7608, 9497. PA 456/1, PA 2124/3/44, PA 2860/1/5, PA 3029/4/3/50

Criminal Statistics England and Wales, 1939-1945, Cmnd 7227, HMSO,1947

Interviews with Gwen Adsley, Ruth Bourne, Pat Field, Vera Stobbs, Rose Parry, Eileen Doxford, Ettore Emanuelli, Evelyn, Jack and Andy Philp, Tom Hutt, Margaret Allen, Leslie Briggs, Pat Field, Tracy Whittlestone, Terry and Winifred Bottrill, Stella Passey, Ilene Hutchinson, Barbara Carter, Mike Gibson, Anne Lewis-Smith and Eric Lever.

Transcripts of Interviews conducted by Jonathan Byrne of the Bletchley Park Trust with BP veterans; Transcripts of interviews conducted by Colin Barber of the Rhydymwyn Valley History Society.

Books and Articles

Raiding Coventry; An Examination of All Air raids on Coventry 1940-42, John Cutler, University of Ireland, 2010.

Royal Ordnance Factory Aycliffe, the Story of the Aycliffe Angels, Fiona Forsyth and Andrew Hutton.

Bomb Girls, Jacky Hyams, John Blake Publishing, 2013

Mother Worked at Avro, Gerald Myers, Compaif Graphics, 1995.

Yeadon Above The Rest, Kenneth B. Cothliff, Croft Publications, 2011

Gas Masks for Goal Posts, Anton Rippon, The History Press, 2005.

The Secret Life of Bletchley Park, Sinclair McKay, Aurum Press, 2010.

Bletchley Park People, Marion Hill, The History Press, 2004.

The Secrets of Station X, Michael Smith, 2011, Biteback Publishing.

Off Duty, Bletchley Park out Station, Gayhurst Manor, Anne Lewis-Smith, Traeth Publications, 2006.

Fields of Deception, Colin Dobinson, Methuen, 2000.

The History of Broadcasting in the United Kingdom, Volume Three, Asa Briggs, Oxford University Press, 1995.

Auntie's War, the BBC during the Second World War, Edward Stourton, Doubleday, 2017.

BBC Engineering, 1922-1972, Edward Pawley, BBC, 1972

Careless Talk: Tensions within British Domestic Propaganda during the Second World War, Jo Fox, University of Durham, 2012.

London's Secret Tubes, Andrew Emmerson, Capital Transport Publishing, 2007.

The London Cage, Helen Fry, Yale University Press, 2017.

Dunkirk, The Men They left Behind, Sean Longden, Constable and Robinson, 2008.

Saving Britain's Art Treasures, N.J. McCamley, Leo Cooper, 2003.

Coventry, Thursday 14 November 1940, Frederick Taylor, Bloomsbury, 2015.

Willesden at War, Volume 2, the Secret Citadels of WW2, Ken Valentine, 1994.

Shadow Factories, David Rogers, Helion, 2016.

British War Production, 1939-1945, Times Publishing, 1945.

Crime in Wartime, Edward Smithies, George Allen and Unwin, 1982.

Civil Liberties in Britain during WW2, Neil Stammers, Palgrave Macmillan, 1984.

Letting the Side Down; British Traitors in the Second World War, Sutton Publishing, 2003.

Secret Underground Cities, N.J. McCamley, Leo Cooper, 1998.

Prisoner of War Camps in Britain During the Second World War, Jon and Diane Sutherland, Golden Guides Press, 2012.

Churchill's Uninvited Guests, Prisoners of War in Britain in WW2, Sophie Jackson, The History Press, 2010.

Cruel Britannia, A Secret History of Torture, Ian Cobain, Portobello Books, 2012.

British Interrogation Techniques in WW2, Sophie Jackson, The History Press, 2011.

Half The Battle, Civilian Morale in Britain during the Second World War, Robert Mackay, Manchester University Press, 2002.

Wartime Britain 1939-1945, Juliet Gardiner, Headline Book Publishing, 2004.

The People's War, Angus Calder, Jonathan Cape, 1969.

Deceiving Hitler, Terry Crowdy, Osprey Publishing, 2008.
The War in The West, James Holland, Transworld Publishers, 2015.
The Secret War, Max Hastings, William Collins, 2015.
A variety of newspaper and magazine articles including *Midland Daily Telegraph, Pearson's Weekly, Liverpool Daily Post, The Times, The Guardian, Daily Mail, Daily Telegraph, BBC People's War, BBC News, Kent Life, Wharfedale and Airedale Observer, Lancashire Life, Subterranea Britannica, Wales Online, Northern Echo, Banbury Times, Newcastle Chronicle.*

Websites

www.aycliffeangels.org.uk
www.munitionsworkers.wordpress.com
www.covfhs.org
www.theherbert.org/history_centre
www.historychristchurch.org.uk/
www.drakelow-tunnels.co.uk
www.hillingdon.gov.uk/bunker
www.liverpoolwarmuseum.co.uk/
www.english-heritage.org.uk/visit/places/dover-castle
www.culture24.org.uk/history-and-heritage/military-history/world-war-two
www.tangmere-museum.org.uk/
www.harringtonmuseum.org.uk/
www.bunker13.co.uk/b13/
www.bentleypriorymuseum.org.uk/
www.nationaltrust.org.uk/hughenden
www.iwm.org.uk/visits/churchill-war-rooms
www.bletchleypark.org.uk
www.mkheritage.co.uk
www.beaumanorhall.co.uk
www.mkars.org.uk/mkars/radio_secret_security_service
www.barnet4u.co.uk
www.purbeckradar.org.uk
www.bawdseyradar.org.uk
www.therocmuseum.org/
www.telegraphmuseum.org
www.stmargarets.london/forum
www.bunkers.org.uk

www.findingshakespeare.co.uk
www.ouseburntrust.org.uk
www.suttonbeauty.org.uk
www.coleshillhouse.com
www.trentparkmuseum.org.uk
www.edencamp.co.uk
www.rhydymwynvalleyhistory.co.uk
www.nationaltrust.org.uk/clumber-park
www.subbrit.org.uk

Acknowledgements

I would like to thank the following people and organisations who have helped with the research and production of this book:

James Taylor, Sebastian Wainwright, Sarah Paterson, Imperial War Museum; Damian Kimberley, Victoria Northridge and Robert Witts, Coventry Archives and Research Centre; Staff at the National Archives, Kew; Staff at the University of York Library; Staff at the University of Leeds Library; Dan Stirland and Andy Stracey, Battle of Britain Bunker Museum at Uxbridge; David Kenyon and Jonathan Byrne, Bletchley Park Trust; Nick Catford and Bill Ridgeway of Subterranea Britannica; Jeff Walden at the BBC Written Archives at Caversham; Staff at the BBC Press Office; Abigail Phillips, Western Approaches Command Museum, Liverpool; Roger Bishop and Colin Anderson of Bunker 13 Newcastle; Rowena Willard-Wright of Dover Castle; Colin Barber of Rhydymwyn Valley History Society, Nina Hannaford of CART (Coleshill Auxiliary Research Team); Andrew Edwards, BBC Radio Leeds; Brody Swain and Elizabeth Rogan, BBC Coventry and Warwickshire; Christchurch Local History Society; Phil Judkins of Purbeck Radar Society; Staff at the ROF59 Activity Centre, Newton Aycliffe; Leigh Calladine, Hilltop Centre, Doncaster; Doncaster Local Studies Centre; Gerald and Nancy Myers; Colin Straw and Paula Jackman of Braithwaite and Jackman Architects; Mick Kelly of Leeds Bradford Airport Industrial Estate; Simon Raine, Wearside Cheeses; Margaret Goodchild, Visit County Durham; Katy Bajina, Network Homes; Andrew Turner; Zoe Hill, Beaumanor Hall; Alex Jackson, National Football Museum; Matthew Taylor, De Montfort University; Ouseburn Trust, Newcastle; St Margaret's Community Forum, Richmond-upon-Thames; Coventry Family History Society; Max Hopkinson, Shapla Halim, Brent Archives; Clifford Wadsworth, Willesden Local History Society; Ann Coxon and Erwyn Jones, Ffestiniog Town Council; Louise Dancy, Halstead Parish Council; Jeff Tutt, Dunkirk Parish Council; Rachel Feldberg, Ilkley Literature Festival; Syima

Aslam and Rebecca Duncan, Bradford Literature Festival and to anyone else who has helped me and whom I have inadvertently overlooked.

As ever my thanks to the team at Pen and Sword including Henry Wilson, Matt Jones, Irene Moore, Jon Wilkinson and Katie Eaton. All images in this book have been credited where possible in the captions. We have made our best efforts to do this accurately from information available and have contacted the rights holders where appropriate and possible.

My particular thanks to those who lived through the Second World War and to their families and who were kind enough to share their experiences with me either directly or through earlier interviews, including Vera Stobbs, Gillian Massey, Alan Francis, Joan Fanshawe, Rose Parry, Gwen Adsley, Ruth Bourne, Eileen Doxford, Ettore Emanuelli, Evelyn, Jack and Andy Philp, Tom Hutt, Margaret Allen, Leslie Briggs, Pat Field, Tracy Whittlestone, Terry and Winifred Bottrill, Stella Passey, Ilene Hutchinson, Barbara Carter, Mike Gibson, Anne Lewis-Smith and Eric Lever.

My special thanks to friends and family members who helped in various ways including Ruth Tompsett, Andrew Rose, Claire Boomer, Paul Richards, Kit Monkman, John Stachiewicz, Alex Philpott, Julia Philpott and Archie Philpott.

Last but not least my very special thanks to Hilary Philpott for proof reading, advice and unfailing support and encouragement.

Index